C000170432

Small Companies, Big Profits

How to make money investing in small companies

Rodney Hobson

HARRIMAN HOUSE LTD

3A Penns Road
Petersfield
Hampshire
GU32 2EW
GREAT BRITAIN

Tel: +44 (0)1730 233870
Fax: +44 (0)1730 233880
Email: enquiries@harriman-house.com
Website: www.harriman-house.com

First published in Great Britain in 2008
Copyright © Harriman House Ltd

The right of Rodney Hobson to be identified as Author has been asserted
in accordance with the Copyright, Design and Patents Act 1988.

ISBN: 978-1905641-78-9

British Library Cataloguing in Publication Data
A CIP catalogue record for this book can be obtained from the British Library.

All rights reserved; no part of this publication may be reproduced, stored in a
retrieval system, or transmitted in any form or by any means, electronic,
mechanical, photocopying, recording, or otherwise without the prior written
permission of the Publisher. This book may not be lent, resold, hired out or
otherwise disposed of
by way of trade in any form of binding or cover other than that in which it is
published without the prior written consent of the Publisher.

Photo of Rodney Hobson by Jamil Shehadeh

Printed and bound by the CPI Group Antony Rowe, Chippenham

No responsibility for loss occasioned to any person or corporate body
acting or refraining to act as a result of reading material in this book
can be accepted by the Publisher or by the Author.

About the author

Rodney Hobson is an experienced financial journalist and author who has held senior editorial positions with publications in the UK and Asia. Among posts he has held are News Editor for the Business Section of *The Times,* Editor of *Shares* magazine, Business Editor of the *Singapore Monitor* and Deputy Business Editor of the *Far Eastern Economic Review.*

Jamil Shehadeh

He has also contributed to the City pages of the *Daily Mail, The Independent* and *The Independent on Sunday.*

Rodney was at the forefront of financial websites, firstly as Head of News for the launch of *Citywire* and more recently as Editor of *Hemscott,* for whom he continues to write a weekly investment email for subscribers.

He is author of *Shares Made Simple*, the authoritative beginner's guide to the stock market, which was published by Harriman House in November 2007.

Rodney is registered as a Representative with the Financial Services Authority. He is married with one daughter.

To Marie Claire

Contents

Preface

What this book covers

This book is about the 2,000 small companies with full listings on the London Stock Exchange (LSE) and another 2,000 whose shares are quoted on the Alternative Investment Market (AIM), the junior branch of the LSE.

That means all the companies on the exchange except the 350 largest ones fall within the purview of our information and analysis.

The book explains how smaller companies differ from larger ones, where to find information on possible investments, the key points to look for and how to assess their prospects. It also highlights the ways in which shareholders can monitor the progress of the companies they invest in.

The buying and selling of smaller company shares is covered but not investment and unit trusts. Nor do I cover the more speculative spheres of contracts for difference and spread betting. Even so, the analysis is useful to those who prefer not to invest directly in shares but who still want a keen grasp of the performance of smaller companies.

Who this book is for

This book is for investors who have some experience of stock market investing and who want to widen their horizons away from large companies offering little excitement and comparatively modest returns. It opens up a whole new world of great investment opportunities, where potential blockbusters lurk below the radar screens of most investors, including City professionals.

It is assumed that readers have a basic knowledge of what shares are and how the stock market works. You should know, for example, how shares are created, what rights the shareholders in a company have, why share prices rise and fall, and what happens when a takeover bid is launched.

However, you do not need a detailed understanding of a balance sheet or fundamental data to understand the information in this book.

Intermediate and advanced investors, as well as comparative beginners, will benefit from the wealth of information and advice. Similarly, it will appeal to long term investors seeking income and capital growth equally as much as to active traders alert to short term gains.

The book concentrates on stock market investing, although spread betters and traders of contracts for difference will widen their knowledge by reading this book. It should be noted that the new forms of trading tend to be available for only the more liquid, heavily traded stocks, and that usually means larger companies.

Finally, this book is for those investors willing to accept greater risk in exchange for the potential for greater returns and who want advice on how to select small companies that will perform while reducing the downside risk. They do not need to have a large sum to invest but they should have some solid investments in their portfolio and be able to stand any losses they may suffer in the pursuit of higher rewards.

Structure of the book

The book is divided into three parts:

- **Part I** defines what small companies are, discusses the various reasons why they are small, and considers the special characteristics that distinguish them from their larger counterparts. It looks at the ways in which small companies are traded on the London Stock Exchange.

- **Part II** gets down to the nitty gritty of analysing and assessing smaller companies, from where to find information to spotting the make or break signs.

- **Part III** has case studies showing how small companies made the grade or fell short of earlier hopes, with lessons for investors highlighted.

Supporting websites

The accompanying website for this book can be found at:
www.harriman-house.com/smallcompanies

Rodney Hobson's personal website is: www.rodneyhobson.co.uk

Introduction

Domino's Pizza – isn't that a downmarket takeaway chain with accident-prone motorcyclists?

Speedy Hire – a group of white van men supplying local builders who can't afford their own equipment?

Ten or 20 years ago those impressions might have been valid, but today there is a different side to these companies. Today these companies stand out as fantastic success stories – as delighted shareholders will readily testify.

Domino's and Speedy are among many UK companies that started out small but ambitious. Those three dots on the Domino's logo? That's the number of outlets it started with. Now the total is heading for 500. Speedy Hire was formed when a single outlet in Wigan took over another three in the North West. It now has national coverage with over 500 outlets and is much more than a humble tool hire company.

They are not alone. Two budget airlines that dared to challenge the world are now bigger than many of the entrenched flag carriers doomed to struggle to satisfy national pride. Ryanair and easyJet started small. Look at them now.

Stagecoach was a regional Scottish bus company inching its way forward in what had been a shrinking sector in the age of the motor car … ICAP found a tiny niche acting as go-between among brokers in the esoteric world of specialist finance … Bloomsbury Publishing put its faith in an unknown author called J. K. Rowling … Hornby revived the dying UK toys industry … Wolseley transformed itself from being a dying car manufacturer into an international building materials group specialising in plumbing equipment … the list goes on and on.

The following table shows the gains that were made investing £1,000 in five small companies on the first trading day of 2001 and selling on the final trading day of 2007. This period has not been selected to inflate the figures. It includes the final two-and-a-quarter years of the last long bear market and the slump in the second half of 2007. In other words, for 40% of the period the stockmarket generally was in freefall.

Company	Buy price	No. shares bought	Sell price	Sale proceeds	Dividends received	Total return
Hornby	28p	3,571	238p	£8,500	£1,414	£9,914
Domino's Pizza	10.5p	9,524	171.75p	£16,357	£2,996	£19,353
Speedy Hire	242.5p	412	838p	£3,456	£354	£3,810
Stagecoach	68.5p	1,460	285p	£4160	£335	£4,495
ICAP	62p	1,613	726.5	£11,717	£851	£12,568

These are the kind of companies that investors dream of and there are plenty more out there waiting to be discovered if you know what to look for.

It is admittedly easy to look on the companies I have highlighted with the wisdom of hindsight but in each case there were signs along the way that these companies were destined for greater things. Some make excellent case studies in Part III and we shall see that, in broad terms, they had strong management; they focused on growing markets or spotted scope for new products or services; they secured a regular long term stream of income; they expanded steadily and purposefully without over extending themselves; in short, they had a clear strategy.

The London stock market is now geared up to giving smaller companies the opportunities to make their mark across the whole range of stock market sectors, including finance, property, electronics, mining, oil, retailing and technology.

Regulation is firm but light, striking a balance between the need to protect investors and the scope to allow smaller companies to thrive. And thrive they do. You might have thought after the stock market slump between 2000 and 2003 that it was the biggest companies that offered the best prospects as shares recovered.

After taking a look at this chart showing how Domino's Pizza performed compared with the FTSE 100 Index, think again.

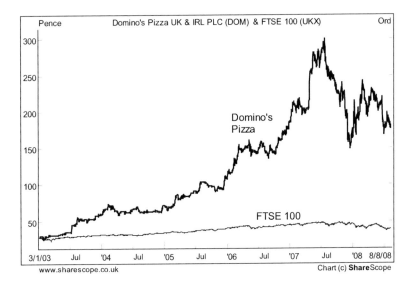

We shall take a closer look at why Domino's did so well over this period later in the book.

It was the tiniest companies that led the way as the stock market powered through more than four years of steadily rising share prices.

FTSE Fledgling (NSX) & FTSE 100 (UKX)

The Fledgling Index comprises companies that are not even large enough to be classified as small! Their outperformance is quite stunning.

Let us be clear: investing in smaller companies is generally more risky than sticking to the top end of the stock market. It can be more difficult to buy and sell shares in companies with fewer shares in issue or where a majority of shares are controlled by a handful of investors.

However, extra risks bring extra potential rewards for those willing to temper bravado with a little diligence and common sense.

Rodney Hobson

August 2008

PART I.
What is a Small Company?

1.
What Is Small?

Different ways of being small

There is no cut and dried definition of what constitutes a small company, but four characteristics are useful to look at:

1. stock market valuation
2. revenue
3. profit
4. number of staff

We shall look at each in turn, assessing their merits as a means of judging potential investments.

1. Stock market valuation

By far the most rational way of judging whether a company is small is to consider the way that the stock market values companies (their *market capitalisations*, or *market caps* for short).

If we multiply the number of shares that a company has issued by the price of the share on the stock market we arrive at the total value the stock market has put on the company. For example, at the time of writing the company Trafficmaster has issued 136 million shares which are trading at 36.25p on the stock market, which gives the company a market cap of £49m. If you wanted to buy the whole company, it would cost you £49m to buy all its shares at the current price.

This valuation changes day by day, sometimes minute by minute, as share prices fluctuate.

An idea of size profile of companies listed on the LSE can be seen with reference to the following table.

Mkt Cap(£m)	Number of companies
>2000	114
500-2000	172
100-500	348
50-100	207
20-50	333
10-20	230
2-10	418

For example, there are 207 companies listed on the LSE with a market cap between £50m and £100m. The data in the table is illustrated graphically in the following chart.

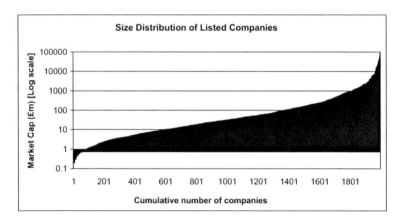

From the chart is can be seen that there are approximately 1400 companies with a market capitalisation below £100m.

Using market cap as a measure of size, we can easily identify a company such as Tesco (market cap: £33bn) as being a big company, and Moss Bros (market cap: £38m) as a small company. This handily correlates with how we would intuitively describe these companies. But the question is:

At what market cap level does a company cease to be small?

The London Stock Exchange has a convenient – if arbitrary – way of drawing that line. The 100 largest companies are regarded as *large caps* – that is, they have the largest stock market capitalisations and they form the FTSE 100 index (sometimes also called the *Footsie*). The next 250 companies are the *midcaps* with middle-sized stock market caps. Anything else is small.

As a rough guide, companies in the Footsie are likely to have a market capitalisation of at least £2.5bn. The figure has been as high as £3bn when the stock market was at its peak. Naturally, the figure varies according to the state of the stock market. The barrier for inclusion in the FTSE 250 index is approximately £300-400m but again the figure can vary considerably with movements in the market generally.

A committee set up by the *Financial Times* and the London Stock Exchange reviews membership of the FTSE 100 and 250 indices every three months so that growing companies can be promoted and shrinking ones moved down.

The main advantage of this definition from an investor's point of view is that it is the stock market's own way of sorting the men from the boys and it is on the stock market that we will be investing. Also, however arbitrary it may be, it is at least a clear and widely accepted classification system. The investment community can all talk the same language.

Problems with this method of classification

The disadvantage is that a specific number of companies are taken to be large or midcap but stocks do not necessarily split up in such a convenient fashion. Also, this division treats all companies traded on AIM as being small, whereas the largest AIM companies are of greater size than many smaller companies with full listings.

AIM is the 'junior' half of the London stock market. As we shall see later, it is less tightly regulated than the main London Stock Exchange and has therefore been able to attract newer, smaller companies that would not qualify for a full stock market listing. However, the biggest companies on AIM are larger than the smallest ones with a full listing. Oil & Gas explorer Sibir Energy would come close to qualifying for the FTSE 100 index if its shares were traded on the main board. Synergy Healthcare and flooring maker James Halstead would be contenders for the FTSE 250.

Stock market valuations can be highly subjective. Share prices are based on assumptions of how well a company is likely to fare over the next two or three years and these assumptions can be wide of the mark. This was particularly in evidence during the tech market boom in the run-up to the new millennium when a clutch of companies, such as Baltimore Technologies, stormed into the Footsie. Many such companies were still small by any reckoning other than market capitalisation and over-inflated sales projections. Some, such as Bookham Technology, Thus and Kingston Communications survived and even thrived as smaller companies after the tech bubble burst.

Nonetheless, market caps provide the most reliable and meaningful way of judging the size of a company as far as investors are concerned and it is the measure that we will rely on most in this book.

Penny shares

One other way of judging a small company based on its stock market price is using the category of penny shares. Some pundits use the term to refer to shares trading at less than 100p, as that means they are worth less than £1 and are thus valued in pennies. However, it is more widely accepted that the term refers to shares trading at 10p or less.

Penny shares can be deceptively attractive to private investors because they look "cheap" and an increase of just a few pence in the share price can easily double the value of a holding. However, they are very much at the high risk/high reward end of the market and such shares should be treated with especial care. We shall look at why this is so in more detail later.

While a company whose shares have sunk below 10p is likely to be small on any other criterion, penny stocks are not necessarily worth less than companies with a higher share price. Construction group Costain with a lowly share price of 24p still managed a stock market valuation of just over £150m, six times the capitalisation of chemicals group Treatt, whose share price was ten times as great at 240p. Cameras retailer Jessops was still worth £7.3m after its shares had slumped to a measly 7p, while industrial engineer Tex was valued at only £6.4m despite its 101p share price.

2. Revenue

The bigger the company, then roughly speaking the greater its sales are likely to be. Revenue is the top line on all company results so we can see easily whether sales are substantial and whether they are rising.

Unlike share prices, which can fluctuate over short periods of time and are at the mercy of the subjective views of investors, all past revenue figures are hard facts and by and large we can judge the continuing sales trend from trading updates issued by the company.

Revenue figures can be distorted if a company specialises in particularly expensive goods or services, for example highly technical equipment. Some sectors are particularly inappropriate for judging in terms of revenue. For instance, a property investment company may sell an entire shopping mall one year and part with no holdings the next year. However, revenue does on the whole provide an objective view of the size of a company.

One point to watch for is that a small company with low turnover can be in danger of being squeezed out of the market by larger rivals. On the other hand, a specialist company with solid sales is potentially a sound investment.

3. Profits

This is the least helpful definition of a small company from an investor's point of view. It is true that small companies will be unlikely to make large profits but large companies can certainly make small profits.

4. Number of staff

This is probably the definition that one can most easily understand. We can readily visualise the self-employed trader, ranging up to a small partnership, to a handful of employees, to a major company with thousands of workers.

Companies with few employees can be tightly run. The boss knows everybody and the employees feel part of the firm, almost as part of a family. Everyone can see the contribution they are making and where they fit in the great scheme of things.

Such businesses can have highly motivated and productive staff.

However, if trading gets tough then a company with few employees cannot cut costs by shedding surplus staff. If assets are, instead, tied up mainly in expensive machinery and premises then any change in revenue will have a magnified effect on profits.

A fall in sales will not be matched by a reduction in costs because assets will be running well below capacity. On the other hand, when times are good it may be easy to step up production.

A company with few staff is likely to be heavily dependent on just one or two of them to act as the driving force. Possibly this is a company run by its founder with a handful of hand-picked supporters. If the founder leaves or is ill then the firm may be rudderless.

A company with a large staff can stand the loss of even quite senior staff. No one is indispensable when there is someone else to step into the departing worker's shoes. The loss of one or two key members of a tightly knit team can be rather more serious.

A small team will have particular difficulty in expanding. It is possible that staff will be overwhelmed by extra work and will be unable to cope if the company tries to diversify, even into related activities.

On the other hand, as long as the team sticks together doing what they do best the company is likely to be successful.

Summary

For the purposes of this book we shall take stock market capitalisations as the main criterion for deciding which companies are small. We shall regard all companies outside the FTSE 100 and FTSE 250 indices, including all stocks quoted on AIM, as our universe. We shall, however, bear in mind the other criteria where this is of particular relevance.

2.
Stock Markets – Where Are Small Companies Traded?

There are four (unequal) arenas where small companies are traded in the UK:

1. LSE Main Market
2. AIM (part of the LSE)
3. PLUS Markets
4. Regional markets

These are looked at in detail below.

LSE Main Market

The main exchange for trading shares in the UK is the London Stock Exchange (LSE). All the biggest companies in the country, and many foreign ones, have their shares traded on what is known as the *Main Board* (even though, in this technological age of trading on computer screens, the share prices are no longer stuck up on a board in a trading room in the exchange).

This is referred to as a *full listing*. It means that companies have complied with strict financial standards, such as having to trade successfully for five years before they can have their shares traded.

A full listing is not, however, the sole prerogative of larger companies. Any company, however small, that complies with the listing requirements and is willing to pay the stock exchange's fee can have a full listing. The big attraction is the prestige attached to being a part of one of the world's premier stock exchanges in one of the world's top financial centres. However, the cost of listing is a deterrent to many small companies.

Many investors, especially funds such as pension funds, hedge funds, unit trusts and investment trusts, will invest only in stocks listed on the main market. It invokes an air of trustworthiness, so suppliers and customers of a listed company will generally feel that it is on solid foundations. After all, the listed company has had to comply with rigorous regulations far in excess of the minimum requirements under European Union law and of a higher standard than most other stock exchanges.

The listed company's name will be more widely known and that may help it to win business.

A company proposing to list on the main market must appoint a sponsor, usually an investment bank, stockbroker or other financial adviser, who will prepare a prospectus containing all the information necessary for a potential investor to decide whether to buy the shares. The company will need a firm of accountants, legal advisers and a registrar to keep the register of shareholders up to date. Most also appoint a public relations consultant.

At least 25% of the shares must be held by persons unconnected with the company, the stock market capitalisation must be at least £700,000 and the company is usually required to have a three year track record.

It costs an estimated £750,000 to float on the main market, including a modest £225 application fee, £5,700 for vetting the prospectus and the rest in fees to advisers. The stockbroker will take 2-5% commission on the money raised in the float. There is an annual stock exchange fee of £3,950 and, for UK companies, an annual financial reporting fee of £4,250.

One can see why many small companies baulk at the cost.

AIM

Since the cost of a full listing is tangible while the benefits are perceptions, perfectly solid, respectable, well run companies can decide to be listed on the Alternative Investment Market (normally referred to by its acronym AIM). AIM has grown rapidly since it was set up in 1995 and it now has well over 2,000 companies. Typically they have a market capitalisation between £2m and £100m and they have raised more than £11 billion between them over the years.

Strictly speaking, companies whose shares are traded on AIM are *quoted*, not *listed*. However, the difference from an investor's point of view is largely technical and the two terms are commonly interchanged.

AIM – often referred to as the LSE's second or junior market – has generally laxer rules, although it does not mean that companies whose shares are traded on AIM can play fast and loose.

Nomads

To join AIM a company must appoint a nominated adviser (*Nomad* in stock market jargon) to check that the company is in good financial shape and to assist in drawing up a prospectus. Nomads are financial advisers approved by and registered with the LSE. Rules governing Nomads are much stricter than for the quoted company itself. It is for the Nomad to ensure that the normal mandatory standards of behaviour one would expect from a quoted company – accounts issued twice a year, annual meetings called and prompt announcements of any takeover approaches or changed profit expectations – are adhered to.

If an AIM company falls out with its Nomad it must appoint a replacement immediately, otherwise its shares will be suspended from trading on the stock market. The most common reason for this happening is that the Nomad is not satisfied that the company is complying fully with the AIM rules. Failure to find a new Nomad will ultimately mean expulsion from AIM. Unfortunately if this happens it is too late for investors to get out as trading in the shares has stopped.

AIM companies also need a stockbroker member of the London Stock Exchange.

There is no minimum level of shares that needs to be held by the public; no trading record is required; and there is no minimum stock market capitalisation.

The London Stock Exchange charges a one-off admission fee of £4,000 for joining AIM but advisers' fees, for the Nomad, solicitors, share registrars, a stock broker and possibly a PR adviser, add £300,000 or more while, as with a full listing, there will be broker's fees of 2-5% of all money raised.

Moving between the main board and AIM

Some companies join AIM in the hope that one day they will grow up and join the big boys on the main board. Successful examples include:

- Support services group **Spice**, which described the move as a coming of age. It cited increased liquidity for the shares, and a belief that it would be taken more seriously in the US, where it was seeking to grow its business, as major reasons.

- Media group **Mecom**, which had grown rapidly into a pan-European business.

- **Hardy Oil & Gas**, the exploration group, which said it had grown considerably during its three years on AIM.

Others used to have a full listing but have stepped down to save money. Examples include:

- Software specialist **Gladstone**, which slimmed down the business after suffering pre-tax losses.

- Textiles group **Dawson International**, which struggled in difficult markets after losing its main customer Marks & Spencer.

- Clothing retailer **Jacques Vert** cited greater flexibility in raising funds and lower costs as reasons for switching from a full listing to AIM.

In general terms, companies moving up the ladder prove better investments both before and after the move than those switching to AIM. The excellent trading that prompts a company to seek a full listing is likely to continue – the implication is that the company would stay on AIM if it was not confident of further improvement – while any problems that push a company to save money on listing costs will not go away of their own accord.

Among the examples given, Hardy Oil went on to achieve inclusion in the FTSE 250 index while Dawson International and Jaques Vert became penny stocks.

Summary

In general companies listed on the main market are bigger than those on AIM – so the latter is an obvious hunting ground for the small company investor. But remember, the range of companies on AIM is wide – the largest AIM companies are almost the same size as those companies at the bottom end of the FTSE 100 Index.

PLUS Markets

There is a third important trading arena called PLUS. This is not part of the London Stock Exchange, although it is also based in London and LSE listed companies can also be traded on PLUS. PLUS is self-regulated but comes under the Financial Services Authority.

Its main role in life is to act as an alternative to AIM. More than 200 smaller companies have their shares quoted on PLUS. Not all stockbrokers operate on this market, though, so if you are interested in making an investment you should check that your broker can oblige.

PLUS does not, as the LSE does, require the issuing of a prospectus before a company can join. Companies that do prepare a prospectus drawn up to accepted standards are eligible to use a streamlined admission procedure.

For applications not accompanied by a prospectus, PLUS will consult an application panel, comprising city practitioners and experts in a range of business sectors including mineral exploration, biotechnology and property.

The panel consultation allows PLUS to make a properly informed assessment of companies operating in a specialist sphere of activity, based on input from panel members with appropriate knowledge and expertise.

Joining PLUS involves an application fee of £5,000 and an annual fee of between £4,000 and £6,500 depending on the company's market capitalisation. A company coming to PLUS will also incur costs from its corporate adviser, solicitors and accountants and any other appropriate advisers involved in the flotation.

Regional exchanges

The UK used to have regional stock markets but these disappeared before London's pre-eminence. It is hard to keep smaller exchanges going because of the difficulty of attracting investors in sufficient numbers to match up buyers and sellers.

However, an attempt has been made to revive the Birmingham Stock Exchange as a forum for small West Midlands companies to raise capital. The new exchange, called *Investbx*, was launched in summer 2007 with the aim of providing investments of between £500,000 and £5m.

Even the sponsor, regional development agency Advantage West Midlands, admitted that Investbx would be "more like eBay than the London Stock Exchange". Shares will be traded online through an auction process that matches buyers and sellers.

Delisting

One question that the smallest companies on the stock market must consider is whether it is worth the annual cost of having their shares traded on the stock exchange.

As well as paying the exchange a fee for this privilege, companies must pay for financial advisers, the maintenance of a share register and for postage when they communicate with shareholders.

Companies quoted on the main stock exchange have the option of reducing costs by moving down to AIM. However, even an AIM quotation costs more than £150,000 a year, which some of the tiniest companies can ill afford.

Quite often when a tiny but successful company wishes to cut out this expense, the management will offer to buy out the other shareholders and take the company private.

On rare occasions, however, a company may feel that its best interests lie in delisting. This is bad news for shareholders, who face being stuck with shares that cannot be sold and may be effectively worthless.

Once a company reveals its intention to delist the share price inevitably falls sharply as shareholders scramble to get out while they still can.

There is a safeguard in that 75% of the shares must be voted in favour of delisting but if management controls a large enough stake it is possible to achieve that figure, especially as many small shareholders vote for whatever management tells them to in a combination of ignorance and blind faith.

Delisted firms usually provide a facility for matching up potential share buyers with existing shareholders who want to sell. However, this is not done through the stock exchange and in reality it will be extremely difficult if not impossible to trade shares.

Case study: Imagesound

The UK's largest provider of piped music in retail stores never fully recovered from a profit warning in mid-2005, just 12 months after it was floated on AIM in August 2004.

Early announcements were positive, with contracts won at Somerfield supermarkets and the B&Q do-it-yourself chain. In March 2005 Imagesound reported a pre-tax loss of £565,000 but it reassured shareholders that after a strong start to the current year it was in line to produce a profit of £1.2m for 2005.

By August a trading statement sought to lower expectations and a month after that interim results showed another loss. In fact, Imagesound made a loss for the full 2006 year and in 2007 the pre-tax loss topped £1m.

Chart 2.1: Imagesound

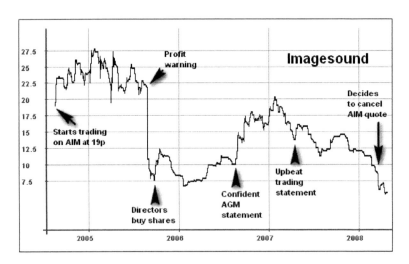

Imagesound shares peaked at 28p early in 2005 but the profit warning sent them crashing from 22.5p to 7.5p and they were as low as 5.5p when the proposal to delist was announced in April 2008.

The company had intended to use its stock market status to raise funds to make acquisitions. The poor share performance meant that debt was used instead, which exacerbated the situation.

This was a very difficult situation for small investors who were lulled by the earlier assurances on trading but it is important to bear in mind that managements are always tempted to put the best gloss on the situation. Where a company does not have a long track record it is right to treat pronouncements with extra caution.

The August trading statement was a clear warning sign and although it was hard for investors to bite the bullet and sell out at a loss the dangers of staying in and losing everything were considerable. Companies that disappoint once usually go on to disappoint again, and again.

Once the company decided to delist there was no point in staying in as the shares would become worthless. Investors needed to get out at whatever price they could get.

Do not be tempted to try to buy shares in this situation as any hope of recovery is very thin indeed.

Key points

- A stock market quotation is not suitable for every company, especially those making losses.

- Newer companies with a full listing are likely to represent a more solid investment than those on AIM or PLUS because the criteria for joining are tougher. However, companies on the junior market are still regulated and must keep investors informed of results and any developments that could affect the share price.

- Companies moving up from PLUS to AIM or from AIM to a full listing are likely to attract the attention of larger investors so their shares are quite likely to rise further.

- It is not a death knell if a company moves down from a full listing to AIM but shareholders should look very carefully at the motives for the move. Is AIM more appropriate or is the company seriously strapped for cash?

- Where the quotation serves no useful purpose, it may be in the company's interests to delist, although that will not suit the shareholders. Resisting plans to delist will simply add to the company's expenses, so shareholders lose either way.

3.
Trading Platforms

Because companies of all sorts and sizes seek to have their shares quoted on the stock market, the London Stock Exchange has created different *trading platforms* – that is, different ways in which buy and sell orders are matched up.

Liquidity

These are based on how liquid the shares are. Liquidity refers to how active the trading in a particular share is. The most liquid shares, such as those in HSBC, BP or Vodafone, see a trade go through almost every second throughout the day. Illiquid shares may see a whole day go by without a single deal being struck.

Smaller companies may be *illiquid*, in other words there are fewer buyers and sellers around, perhaps because there are fewer shares in issue, or the company is little known and does not attract the interest of investors, or perhaps large blocks of shares are in the hands or a few major investors who rarely sell.

Different trading systems have evolved in the electronic age to reflect these different levels of liquidity.

SETS

The largest companies on the London Stock Exchange, including all those in the FTSE 100 and the most actively traded FTSE 250 stocks, trade on SETS, the electronic order book. This is the most up-to-date of the trading systems and by far the most efficient and open in matching buyers and sellers.

If you want to buy, your broker will post your bid price and the number of shares you are looking for on to the trading system from his office computer. If you want to sell, your offer price and number of shares for sale are similarly posted.

When a buyer and a seller post the same price, the two are automatically matched up. If, say, the buyer wants 2,000 shares and the seller is offering 3,000 shares, the deal is struck for 2,000 shares (the lower figure) and a sale offer for 1,000 shares remains on the site.

Anyone with access to the trading system – and even a private investor can see the prices displayed on certain financial websites for a subscription fee – is able to see not only the best buying and selling prices available but also how many buy or sell orders have been posted and at what prices.

A clear picture can thus be gained of whether one side outnumbers the other and the sort of levels at which buyers would start to bail out if the share price rises, or where supporters would pile in if the price falls.

The system used on SETS shares is called *order driven*. A broker places orders giving the number of shares you wish to trade and the price at which you are prepared to trade. All the outstanding orders appear in two columns (bid and offer). When the seller offering the highest price and the buyer willing to accept the lowest price match up, a deal is done and these orders disappear from the screen.

SETSmm

There is a hybrid system called SETSmm where the electronic order book is supported by market making so that buy and sell prices are available to investors in medium sized and many smaller stocks.

If trading in a company on SETSmm dries up at any time, market makers will guarantee to buy and sell your shares at the prices they post on screen.

All members of the FTSE midcap index that are not traded on SETS are included along with all those in the Small Cap index, other reasonably liquid stocks on the main board and the more liquid AIM stocks.

Irish companies with a dual listing in London and Dublin are traded on SETSmm.

SEAQ

About 2,000 smaller UK companies on the main market and AIM are traded on SEAQ. This trading platform is for companies that are not sufficiently liquid to be traded on SETS because there would be times when no buy or sell offers were posted and trading would grind to a halt.

Instead, at least two market makers guarantee to post buy and sell prices throughout stock exchange trading hours.

The SEAQ system is called *quote driven*. Market makers quote the prices at which they are prepared to buy and sell and you decide if you want to deal at that price.

On the SEAQ screen there are therefore no columns of buy and sell orders. Instead there is a list of market makers who are prepared to buy and sell stock. Against each market maker is the price at which they will buy and the price at which they will sell. After that is the maximum number of shares, in thousands, they will buy or sell at the price they are quoting.

Market makers are obliged, except in extreme cases, to offer prices on every share in which they make a market during the hours that the Stock Exchange is open. They are obliged to trade at the prices they quote.

The quotes for a particular company will tend to be similar for all market makers in that stock but the quotes may not be identical. If they are, it does not particularly matter which market maker your broker goes to.

However, when a market maker buys in stock it will tend to raise its buy and sell prices; when it sells stock it will lower its price quotes. This is because market makers aim to keep a small amount of stock on their books. To hold a large amount of stock in a rarely traded company would pointlessly tie up capital; to hold no shares would be embarrassing when buy orders come in. So the market maker will adjust prices after each deal to try to keep its books balanced.

SEATS Plus

This service covers the least liquid stocks on the main market and on AIM, where there is only one market maker or possibly none. Either the market maker will be obliged to quote buy and sell prices or your broker will take your order and try to match it with an opposite buy or sell order placed by another investor.

SETS and SEAQ screens

Your broker will have access to Level 2 on the London Stock Exchange. While Level 1 provides basic information such as the best buy and sell prices, Level 2 has much more detailed information that is vital to your broker.

Subscribers to the LSE pay a higher fee for access to Level 2; if you are a serious investor the MoneyAM and ADVFN websites provide Level 2 for their subscribers.

Across the screen will be a yellow band displaying the one thing you really need to know: the best buying price on offer and the best selling price. The gap between the two is known as the spread. These are the prices that your broker will quote to you.

4.

Stock Market Indices

There are many indices created to let the investor know how the stock market in general – and how each of the various different sections of the market – is performing. The most widely followed index in the UK is probably the FTSE 100 Index, which measures the performance of the shares of the largest 100 companies listed on the LSE. But there are many others. Many are compiled by FTSE International, a company jointly owned by the Financial Times and the LSE (hence the name, FTSE: Financial Times Stock Exchange).

The FTSE Family

The main indices of interest to investors are described briefly below.

FTSE 100

The index comprises 100 of the top capitalised stocks listed on the LSE, and represents approximately 80% of the total market (by capitalisation). It is weighted on the basis of market capitalisations. The index was first calculated on 3 January 1984 with a base value of 1000.

FTSE 250

Similar in construction to the FTSE 100, except it comprises the next 250 highest capitalised stocks listed on the LSE after the top 100. The index is sometimes referred to as the index of mid-capitalised stocks (or *mid-caps*) and comprises approximately 18% of the total market capitalisation.

FTSE 350

Similar in construction to the FTSE 100, but including all the companies from the FTSE 100 and FTSE 250 indices.

FTSE Small Cap

Comprised of companies with a market capitalisation below the FTSE 250, but above a fixed limit. In mid-2008 the smallest members of the index had a capitalisation of approximately £50m. Consequently the FTSE Small Cap Index does not have a fixed number of constituents. In mid-2008, there were approximately 293 companies in the index, which represented about 2% of the total market by capitalisation.

FTSE All-Share

The FTSE All-Share is the aggregation of the FTSE 100, FTSE 250 and FTSE Small Cap indices. Effectively all those LSE listed companies with a market capitalisation above the lower limit for inclusion in the FTSE Small Cap Index. In mid-2008, there were approximately 643 companies in the index. The FTSE All-Share Index is the standard benchmark for measuring the performance of the broad UK market.

FTSE Fledgling

This index comprises the smallest companies that do not meet the minimum size requirement of the FTSE Small Cap Index.

FTSE TMT

Reflects the performance of companies in the Technology, Media and Telecommunications sectors.

FTSE techMARK All-Share

An index of all companies included in the LSE's techMARK sector.

FTSE techMARK 100

The top 100 companies of the FTSE techMARK All-Share, under £4bn by full market capitalisation.

FTSE AIM

The index that includes all companies quoted on AIM, including foreign based companies.

FTSE AIM 100

The 100 largest companies on AIM.

FTSE UK 50

The 50 largest UK-based companies on AIM.

Small company investors

If you are looking to invest in smaller companies you will immediately wish to dismiss all occupants of the FTSE 100 index. Immediately below the FTSE 100 is the FTSE 250, which covers the next 250 medium sized companies. Most small company investors would ignore these companies as well.

The FTSE Small Cap index covers the smaller (but not the smallest) companies with a stock market listing. Smaller still are the companies in the FTSE Fledgling index. These are not included in any other index.

Index reviews

Every three months (early in March, June, September and December, always on a Wednesday) a FTSE committee meets to review the composition of the indices, and – according to the rules – may eject or add stocks from/to the range of indices.

Which companies go into which index will depend on stock market capitalisations at the close of trading on the previous evening. Any changes agreed on will be made over the weekend that falls 10 days later, so some companies will end the week in one index and start the next week with a new status.

While movement between the midcaps and the FTSE 100 elite tends to be restricted, with no more than two changes as the norm and no change at all in some quarters, the dividing line between midcaps and small caps is much more fluid. It is not unusual to see half a dozen changes at this level.

This situation presents investment opportunities. Although some large funds will invest only in FTSE 100 stocks, there are others that track the FTSE 250. Tracker funds aim to replicate the performance of a specific index, so FTSE 250 trackers will aim to build and hold a portfolio of those stocks that are included in the midcap index.

Funds are likely to pick up shares in small cap companies that look likely to gain promotion because their market capitalisations are higher than the smallest midcaps. This buying gives the rising stars extra momentum and provides a reward for longer term shareholders.

Index performance

The indices will over time tend to move in roughly the same direction but this is not always the case. Over several months it is quite possible for the smaller end of the market to outperform the big guns.

Investors can compare market indices to see if smaller shares are currently in favour or if they have been left behind and could have some catching up to do.

The following chart shows the comparative performance of three indices: FTSE 100, Small Cap and AIM. The values of the respective indices have been re-based to start at 100, to allow the indices to be shown on the same chart and for a direct performance comparison to be made.

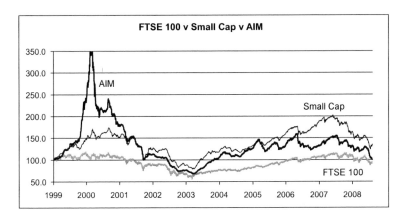

As can be seen in the chart above, from 1999 AIM shares (on average – as measured by the AIM Index) greatly out-performed shares in the FTSE 100 and Small Cap indices. This was during the internet boom when shares in small companies soared. When the boom ended, all shares fell, with the shares of smaller companies falling the most. By the bottom of the bear market in 2003, the Small Cap Index had ended up out-performing the other two indices (from the perspective of an investment made at the beginning of 1999).

The following chart is similar to the above but it focuses on the 2003-2008 period.

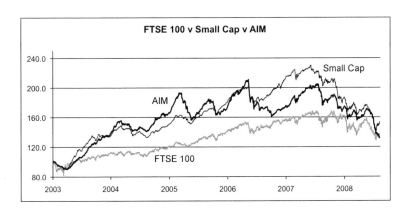

When the stock market started rising again in 2003, after the 2000-2003 bear market, the chart shows that it was the small stocks that raced ahead, leaving behind the large companies in the FTSE 100 Index. On average, Small Cap and AIM stocks performed similarly, until mid-2006, when AIM stocks suffered worst in the brief May 2006 market correction. By June 2007, the FTSE 100 Index had increased 66% from the low in 2003, the AIM Index was up 102%, but the star was the Small Cap Index which had risen 130%. When markets turned down, it was the smaller stocks that started falling first, and fell the most.

The charts clearly illustrate the greater volatility of the smaller stocks – representing risk…and opportunity.

Relative performance

It is useful to compare the performance of companies with a related index.

For example, the following chart shows the price performance of Ennstone, the aggregates producer, over the period March 2003 to May 2006.

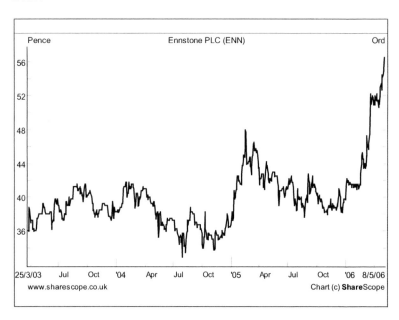

At first glance, the performance looks fine. The shares rose from 36p to 56p – a rise of 56% over the period. An investor, having put some money into Ennstone in March 2003, might be feeling quite pleased with themselves.

However, now look at the following chart.

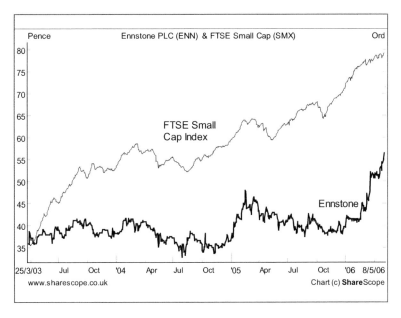

This chart compares the performance of Ennstone with the FTSE Small Cap index over the same period. While Ennstone rose 56%, the Index increased 119%. So, in fact, Ennstone had *underperformed* small cap stocks (generally as measured by the FTSE Small Cap Index) and therefore the investor should not be feeling too pleased with him or herself.

When comparing stock performance with indices, it is important to select the most appropriate index. In this case, the FTSE Small Cap Index was chosen because Ennstone is included in that index. But if one wanted to measure the relative performance of, say, Majestic Wine then the AIM Index may be better as that company is included in the AIM Index.

Sector indices

As well as the standard market-wide indices, there is also a range of indices covering various stock market sectors so you can compare how a company is performing against its peers. You can also see which sectors of the stock market are performing well and which are lagging.

PART II.
Investing in Small Companies

5.

Acorns To Oaks

Companies rarely stand still, whatever their size.

That is good news for investors in smaller companies because it means that there are a great many potential growth stocks at the lower end of the market. Growth, that is, in terms of improving profits and rising share prices.

Most entrepreneurs are, by their very nature, ambitious for the companies that they bring to market. Why go through the hassle of a stock market listing if you prefer the quiet life, jogging along in a backwater?

So, many small companies will be looking for the opportunity to expand. Companies usually raise cash for the business when they join the stock market. Small companies are likely to be able to raise only small amounts of cash, especially in the early days, as big institutional investors are reluctant to take risks with comparatively unknown and untested companies.

It is therefore important to assess whether a small ambitious company has sufficient cash to fulfil its plans and whether its operations are burning up that cash or generating more cash for expansion.

Does the company have clear, sensible plans for using the cash it does have? Will it be able to expand without biting off more than it can chew?

To get a feel of what is involved in taking a start-up company all the way through to being among the largest in the country, let us look at the history of one of the country's success stories.

Case study: Speedy Hire

One of the greatest tales of a tiny company growing into a national giant, rewarding shareholders handsomely along the way, is Speedy Hire.

Formed in 1977 as Livesey Hire with one depot in Wigan, Speedy Hire began life as a privately-owned tool hire company. It was five years before the Speedy name was adopted, when managing director John Brown bought Speedy Fixings Power Tools with three hire outlets in Prescot, Manchester and Llandudno.

The depot network started to grow, following a pattern of adding a mixture of greenfield sites opened by the company and small acquisitions that could be easily absorbed. Wherever possible, existing management of acquired businesses were kept on to provide continuity.

This proved a potent mix. Over the next few years Speedy Hire was able to grow at a steady rate, never overstretching itself. Greenfield start-ups were generally cheaper but took longer to build-up; existing businesses were more expensive per site but already had a clientele.

Speedy grew initially within the North West, spreading gradually outwards from its Wigan base so that, geographically as well as financially, it was never overstretched. Becoming a regional operator had its advantages because North West regional businesses needing to hire tools could always find a Speedy Hire outlet within reach. The first London depot was not opened until 1987.

This gradual expansion was particular important in what was – and still is today – a highly fragmented sector full of small hire companies with no more than a handful of outlets each. This fragmentation also meant that Speedy Hire could be choosy in picking rivals to acquire. If the price demanded by the existing owner was too high, it could walk away and look elsewhere.

Stock market flotation

Meanwhile the private owners of Speedy Hire had wider ambitions and they expanded into construction, civil engineering, property investment and services to utility companies under the group name of Allen plc. In 1989 Allen was floated on the London Stock Exchange, raising funds to finance the growing dream.

A year later, a crucial appointment was made: Steve Corcoran, subsequently to become chief operating officer and a driving force behind continued expansion, joined as a member of the sales team.

As part of a listed company, Speedy Hire gathered pace and the acquisition of Kendrick Hire's 41 branches in September 1994 doubled its size, creating a genuine presence in the south of England, and formed the basis of a nationwide operation.

Even at that stage, though, Speedy Hire was still essentially a small company with fewer than 100 depots, no presence in Scotland and huge gaps in the Midlands, the South West and Wales. These gaps were gradually filled over the 1990s and into the new millennium as it became increasingly clear that Speedy was the driving force behind the entire group. The other operations, some of them loss-making, were sold off in 2001 and the name of the group was changed to Speedy Hire. It was a classic case of sticking to what you do best.

Speedy Hire evolves

In place of the ragbag of ill-assorted, ill-fitting companies that Allen had been, Speedy then began to spread into genuinely related businesses such as lifting equipment, to provide a broader service to its business customers. It set out clear objectives, for example specifying the number of depots it intended to open each year.

The group is now a leading provider of equipment hire services to UK contractors and builders, industry, utilities and the public sector, operating from over 500 depots throughout the country.

Apart from its traditional tool hire, it also has complementary businesses specialising in portable accommodation, lifting, surveying, compressed air systems, pumping and power generation equipment. Its ambitious aim is to be number one in every sector in which it operates.

The increased demands of health and safety have worked in Speedy Hire's favour. The construction industry has in the past had a particularly poor reputation on safety and has increasingly come under pressure to improve its record.

Speedy Hire has constantly renewed its equipment and vehicle fleet, ensuring that the average age of its supplies are among the lowest in the hire sector. Because its equipment is in heavy use, this is economically viable. It makes sense for contractors to hire expensive equipment meeting the latest safety requirements rather than having to constantly renew their own stock.

Chart 5.1: Speedy Hire

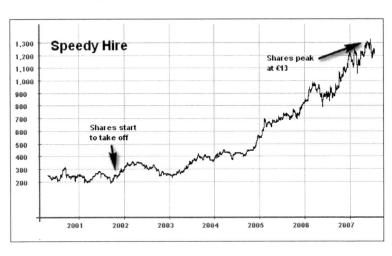

It took time for Speedy Hire shares to take off, for various reasons. As a small but unproven company back in the 1990s it was still largely unknown and attracted little interest from larger investors. Cash was ploughed into growing the business rather than being paid in dividends, so the shares were of no interest to investors seeking income.

However, after finding a floor around 200p in 2000 and 2001, the shares gathered momentum as turnover and profits increased and they hit a peak of 1,300p in the middle of 2007, by which time Speedy Hire had risen to the ranks of medium sized companies. It was included in the FTSE 250 index in June 2006.

Key points

- Ambition works best when it is tempered with reality. Speedy Hire did not try to grow too quickly, sensibly preferring bite size acquisitions rather than indigestible chunks that would overstretch management. It did make some sizeable transactions but these were carefully selected and well spaced out.

- Growing companies need strong, able management.

- A successful track record inspires confidence among suppliers and customers as well as investors.

- Companies that supply goods or services to other businesses benefit from being a one-stop shop. If they have a good reputation they can be used for a range of products across the country.

- Companies may be torn between putting cash into expansion and rewarding shareholders with a dividend. It can be tricky balancing the two needs.

6.
Getting Information

News from the company

The best source of information in identifying small companies to invest in is the company itself.

Most small companies have a website explaining what they do, possibly a brief history of the company and most certainly their recent stock market announcements including company results. Look for buttons on the website with labels such as:

- About us

- Investor Relations

- Recent announcements

- Press releases

Companies with a full listing are not obliged to maintain a website but if they do have one it must be accurate. They cannot, for example, choose to post only favourable stock market announcements on it and suppress profit warnings. Companies quoted on AIM must have a website – this is a rare example of the rules for AIM companies being more onerous than for a full listing.

The website will include a copy of the latest annual report and possibly those for previous years.

Direct contact

One great advantage that smaller companies have from an investor's perspective is that it is often possible to directly contact the chief executive, finance director or company secretary on the phone.

It doesn't always work but if you have a query you can sometimes ring the switchboard and be put straight through. Executives of smaller companies tend to appreciate their shareholders more and will often try to be helpful in answering queries. Have specific questions ready before you ring up and get to the point. Executives are busy people.

Alternatively the company is likely to employ public relations consultants. The name of the PR, and the individuals handling the account, are usually found on stock market announcements on the company website. Getting information from the PR is likely to be less satisfactory than approaching the company directly but most are pretty clued up on the companies they represent.

AGM

Even the most bashful company is obliged to face its shareholders once a year, at the annual general meeting (AGM), which will be called some time in the weeks after the financial year end. The company must inform all shareholders in advance of the time, date and place of the meeting. This is an excellent opportunity to express your opinion, to elicit information and to criticise the directors if the meeting is held at a time and place convenient to you.

This opportunity is much greater in the case of smaller rather than larger companies. Fewer investors turn up to the AGMs of small companies and the large institutional investors are generally absent, so the floor is open. Don't be overawed. This is your company and there will not be many shareholders around if you get flustered at your first attempt.

While these meetings are strictly for shareholders, it is often possible for non-shareholders to sneak in. Smaller companies are often only too pleased to see extra faces – rather than have the platform outnumber the floor. Even if you are rumbled, you will probably be allowed to attend on the understanding that you cannot ask questions or vote. At least you will hear news from the horse's mouth and should have the opportunity to nobble directors afterwards.

Company results

All companies are obliged to issue company results for the half year and full year and most, including all companies with a full listing, also put out routine quarterly management statements indicating if there has been any change in trading since the last figures.

Companies must warn the market if profits are likely to be substantially greater or less than previous expectations.

These announcements are made through the London Stock Exchange's Regulatory News Services (RNS). They must be posted immediately on the company website if it has one.

Companies know in advance when they are announcing results or issuing trading statements, since the directors meet the day before to approve them. Such announcements are routinely made at 7am as the stock market opens but before trading starts. News that directors or large shareholders have bought or sold shares tend to filter through later in the day as these do not usually have as great an impact on a company's share price.

Unfortunately companies are no longer obliged to say in advance when they will be putting out their results, and many small companies no longer bother to do so. As these announcements can affect the share price significantly, especially in the case of a company whose shares are thinly traded, it is important to be alert to imminent announcements.

Results for each company are usually issued on or around the same day each year so you can watch out for them. Where results are delayed, the longer the delay the more likely it is that the news will be bad. Companies are naturally keener to get good news out into the open – whatever the stock exchange rules may say.

Note that AGMs usually include an update on trading and all shareholders must be informed when these are to be held as they have the right to attend. The trading update is usually also issued through the RNS before start of trading on the day that the meeting is held.

Several websites, including Hemscott, Digital Look, InvestEgate and ADVFN, carry all RNS announcements accessible by non-subscribers, though it may be possible to get only that day's announcements free. Look for a button that says something like 'Today's company news' or 'All today's RNS announcements'.

London Stock Exchange

A comprehensive report on all listed and quoted companies is available on the London Stock Exchange website (www.londonstockexchange.com) in the Investor Centre. Useful buttons are Education and Tools.

The company profiles are free and can be read on site or downloaded in a PDF file onto your own computer. In addition to background information on what the company does and who its directors and advisers are, they contain vital information such as normal market share (shown, slightly confusingly, in the report as exchange market share), buying and selling of company shares by directors, the last ten stock market trades in the company shares, trading volumes, broker forecasts and recommendations, and a chart showing how the shares have performed over the past year in comparison with the FTSE 100 index.

Company news from newspapers

City news appears in most newspapers and in specialist magazines. Among newspapers, the widest coverage is inevitably in the *Financial Times*, which devotes easily the most space to business and City news, although it offers little if anything in the way of share tips.

While larger companies dominate, smaller ones are given prominence when their news merits it. The *FT* does have a small section specifically covering announcements by smaller companies on most days, although each report is usually only three paragraphs.

Serious investors may feel that £1.50 a day is not too much to pay for keeping abreast of the whole market but it does mount up and most people require a wider news coverage and will end up buying a national newspaper as well.

The Times, *Daily Telegraph*, *Independent*, *Daily Mail* and the *Daily Express* contain City news coverage but inevitably it is the smaller end of the market that gets left out once the space is filled. The sensible thing is to try different newspapers to decide which one suits you.

Newspapers are particularly useful in alerting readers to imminent results announcements. A list of the week's expected results appears in the more serious Sunday and Monday newspapers. Note that newspapers with less space may print a condensed list at busy times which will inevitably squeeze out the smaller companies. The best lists are in the *FT*, *The Times*, *Daily Telegraph* and *The Independent* on a Monday morning.

Share tips

Share tips as well as news appear in several newspapers and magazines and although there is a preponderance of larger companies, which is understandable given that these are the more heavily traded shares, there is coverage of smaller companies.

By far the heaviest coverage of smaller companies is in the two specialist investment magazines, *Investors Chronicle* and *Shares*. These tend to report results of all but the tiniest companies, adding a potted assessment of the outlook for each company, and they also contain the heaviest concentration of share tips.

The *IC* typically has three or four smaller companies within its tips section. While the corresponding section in *Shares* magazine, Plays of the Week, tends to cover only a couple of shares each week in total, a high proportion are smaller companies. This is because this section is looking for companies with the potential to produce significant growth in a short space of time.

It is cheaper to buy these magazines on subscription, to be posted to your home address weekly, than to buy them on the news stands. The disadvantage of a subscription is that you are relying on the post and it is usually possible to buy a newsstand copy earlier, before everyone else has seen the tips.

Share tips appear daily in the Tempus column in *The Times*, the *Daily Telegraph's* Questor section and in *The Independent*. Again, these are mainly larger companies but you will find some smaller companies – it's just a bit expensive to buy three newspapers every day on the off chance that you will find one smaller company tipped somewhere among them.

Note that the above columns do not appear on Mondays, nor do they appear on Tuesdays immediately after a bank holiday.

There are some share tips to be found in Saturday and Sunday newspapers. The *Daily Mail* runs an Investment Extra column on Saturday and *The Times* contains tips on smaller companies.

Sunday newspapers generally avoid tips columns these days but the Midas column in the *Mail on Sunday* usually covers a couple of stocks, often smaller ones, and the *Sunday Telegraph* tips half a dozen companies, including a fair selection of small companies.

The advantage of weekend share tips is that they are made while the market is closed. It may be possible to put in a buy or sell order with your broker first thing on Monday morning before share prices have moved too far, but always stipulate a limit price because spreads tend to be wider in early trading.

The *Daily Telegraph* has a weekly report on the AIM market on Monday mornings. The *Financial Times* has a stock market report on smaller companies alongside its main stock market report after each trading day on the LSE. This does often contain midcaps.

Broker analysis

Some stockbrokers employ analysts to produce reports on companies or industry sectors for their clients. If you want the benefit of expert advice then trade through a broker that specialises in providing analysis of smaller companies. Note that there will be a fee for this on top of the fee for buying and selling shares.

Stockbrokers specialising in small cap and fledgling companies include Numis Securities, Panmure Gordon, Brewin Dolphin, Arbuthnot Securities, Blue Oar Securities and Evolution Securities.

The three brokers dominating the ranks of AIM companies are Collins Stewart, Seymour Pierce and KBC Peel Hunt.

Unfortunately, most analysis is produced on larger companies; coverage of smaller companies is patchy. Several newspapers including the *Financial Times*, *The Times*, the *Daily Telegraph* and the *Daily Mail* include a summary of the week's analyst reports in their Saturday editions although the majority will be on larger companies.

Broker analysis on smaller companies needs to be treated with extra caution. While the wide range of research on large companies guarantees that some coverage is independent, much research on smaller companies is issued only by the company's own broker. The broker is obliged to declare any connection with the companies it covers. It is especially important to be suspicious of 'hold' recommendations from an in-house broker as few will risk going so far as to say sell for fear of losing business.

LSE - PSQ Analytics

The London Stock Exchange announced that it was setting up a new service, PSQ Analytics, to offer equity research on smaller quoted companies starting in autumn 2008. Companies on AIM, as well as smaller companies on the main market, would be able to pay for independent research to be carried out by three research providers: Independent International Investment Research based in the UK, Argus Research based in New York and Pipal Research based in Chicago. These were to provide standardised research in an agreed template.

The LSE says:

> The three providers all have a strong track record of providing objective research across a wide variety of sectors and will provide information that improves investor understanding of their businesses.

The research is being distributed free of charge through financial news wire services Bloomberg and Thomson Reuters and also on a dedicated website.

This extra information is certainly welcome but investors will need to bear in mind that however independent the research companies are they are still being paid by the company they are researching.

Web sites

The Hargreaves Lansdown website (www.h-l.co.uk) contains its own analysis and a selection of reports from other brokers. Access is free.

Growth Company Investor's website is www.smallcompanies.co.uk with useful sections on news and comment, recommendations and research and analysis.

Timesonline.co.uk includes the Tempus column under business and markets.

On telegraph.co.uk there is a link to Questor through business and companies & markets.

In the business section of independent.co.uk you will find the Investment Column under sharewatch.

Hemscott.com has guidance under news and comment.

The Motley Fool website fool.co.uk is more oriented to personal finance but try clicking on latest stories then fool articles.

Citywire.co.uk has a personal investor section including give me the news.

Investegate.co.uk carries RNS announcements and brokers recommendations.

Thisismoney.co.uk has City news and comment from the *Daily Mail* and the *Mail on Sunday*. You can register free to receive a weekly tips email.

Interactive Investor's website iii.co.uk has videos giving share tips through its iBall TV facility.

7.

Assessing Companies

Now we know where to find information, the big issue is: *what are we looking for?*

Company questions

Consider the following questions:

1. How many products does the company have?

2. Is there revenue from sales?

3. Are sales increasing?

4. Are sales guaranteed to continue into next year and beyond (often referred to as *visibility of earnings*)?

5. Is there a profit after allowing for interest payments and depreciation of assets?

6. Are profits increasing?

7. Are costs under control?

8. Does it have cash, or available unused loan facilities, to carry it over a difficult period?

9. Does the company and its management have a good track record?

10. Is there at least one non-executive director, preferably the chairman, with strong experience at other companies in the sector?

11. Does the company have a clear strategy?

12. Has it carved out a niche market for itself where it will be hard for rivals to set up in competition?

The more of these questions that can be answered with a yes, the more worthwhile it is to consider investing in the company.

On the other hand, a yes to any of the following questions is a warning signal:

1. Is the company heavily in debt?

2. Has it run up a series of pre-tax losses that will prevent it from paying a dividend?

3. Has it issued a profit warning within the past 12 months?

4. Does it have larger rivals providing the same goods and services?

The answers to these questions can be found primarily in facts and figures issued by the company itself: the profit & loss account (or *income statement* as it is increasingly called), the balance sheet and the annual report. These should all be available on the company's own website. If the company does not have a website or it does not, for example, include the annual report, you should be wary of investing in the company.

All AIM-quoted companies must have a website and in this day and age there really is no excuse for a fully listed company not to have one. Shareholders and prospective investors are entitled to full, accurate disclosure of pertinent information.

Income statement and balance sheet

The income statement gives us a rundown on how the company has performed over a specific period of time, either six months or a year; the balance sheet tells us the state of the finances at a given point in time. Together they form the company results.

Both are full of vital information on key issues such as sales, profits, dividends, debt and cash flow, as we shall see in detail in the following two chapters. It is essential to be able to pick out the key figures from the mass of data and to understand whether the company is improving its performance or has serious problems to contend with.

One word of caution. Companies large and small usually issue a helpful summary of the key points but these should always be treated with a pinch of salt. Naturally, the best gloss that can be put on the figures will appear in the statement.

Fortunately statements for smaller companies tend to be much shorter than the self-indulgent waffle you often get from larger ones so there is no excuse for failing to read through to see if anything nasty is hidden lower down the summary before you rush to buy the shares.

Even then, look at the figures in the income statement and balance sheet to see for yourself if there is anything of significance that the company has not deigned to mention.

8.

Income Statement

When do results come out?

Income statements, formerly known as the *profit and loss account*, are published twice a year. The *interim statement* covers the first six months of the financial year and the *final statement* covers the full year. This is standard practice although there may be small variations which are no cause for alarm. For instance, retailers usually issue statements for 26 and 52 weeks rather than for 12 calendar months so that each period contains the same number of trading days.

The timing of the statements naturally depends on the end of the financial year, which is usually 31 December or 31 March. However, there is again no cause for concern if a company has a different date. This may be to avoid having to produce results in a busy trading period.

Only a few larger companies such as Shell and BP produce quarterly income statements – because they have operations in the United States, where results are published four times a year. Do not expect smaller companies to waste money on drawing up their accounts twice as often as they need to, although even small companies now issue quarterly updates that give an overall view of current trading without the detailed figures.

Smaller companies generally take longer to produce their figures after the period end. Larger companies have larger finance departments and can throw resources at drawing up accounts quickly. Nonetheless, smaller companies should be able to pull the figures together well within three months. After all, they have fewer figures to pull together.

Any company's website will have the day of the release of results a year ago. It is therefore easy to see when the next results are expected and to be alert to any delay. Large companies very rarely delay such announcements and the same goes for small companies doing well. As noted earlier, any delay almost invariably is a portent of bad news.

Company results are published through the stock exchange, usually at 7am before trading begins, and can be found on financial news websites within minutes, however small the company. They are also published on the company's own website on the morning of issue.

What do income statements contain?

Revenue

Is the company actually selling anything and are sales increasing at a manageable rate? New companies do quite often come to the stock market to raise money to fund the development of their products so turnover may be low or non-existent. In that case, see what the company has said about when its products will be ready for marketing and consider whether the plans are realistic. Remember the dotcom boom – small companies with no sales collapsed before they could start earning money.

Assuming that revenue does exist, are sales improving, stagnating or slipping? If they are down on the previous year, check if the company offers any credible explanation. Any claims that sales have been merely deferred and will show up in the following year should be treated with particular scepticism. 'Deferred' sales often turn out to be lost sales, another lesson to be learnt from the dotcom days.

It is possible that sales are down because part of the business has been closed or sold but this is less likely in a smaller company as there is less to dispose of. Again, see if the summary offers a plausible explanation, bearing in mind that a smaller company getting smaller is unlikely to prove a worthwhile investment.

Rising sales, on the other hand, offer prospects of rising profits and a rising share price. Steadily growing companies offer the best prospects for rising share prices and dividends over a long term.

Be wary, though, of small companies growing rapidly. Management may become overstretched. Such companies tend to see their shares soar over several months or even years then fall back equally sharply as the bubble bursts. One example was cake maker Inter-Link Foods, which grew by increasing its own sales and buying rival companies. Out of the blue it found it did not have sufficient cash reserves to keep going and went bust instead.

Cost of sales

This line represents the cost of raw materials and labour that went into producing the goods or services the company sells.

These should not be rising faster than sales – if they are then extra sales are being won at a loss. It may be reasonable for a small company to spend heavily to gain a foothold in the market but once again we would want a plausible explanation of why the company is spending so heavily to move forwards and how soon the situation is expected to be reversed.

Administrative expenses

Also referred to as *overheads* or *central costs*, these show how much the company is spending on head office, administration and sales staff. Small companies should have correspondingly small overheads. If these costs approach or exceed cost of sales or seem to be swallowing up a large proportion of revenue then it looks as if the company is top heavy with management.

As with cost of sales, admin should not be rising faster than revenue. Indeed, one would expect a small growing company to increase its central costs quite slowly. Admin has had to be put in place to get the company going. After the start-up, sales should be coming through while admin needs little addition.

Interest

It is perfectly reasonable for small companies to borrow money to start up and/or expand but like all borrowers they need to live within their means. Smaller companies do not have the financial clout that large companies have so borrowing terms may be tough.

Check that there is enough profit after costs are deducted from revenue to fully cover interest payments; otherwise the company is not paying its way. While large companies may be able to ride out a temporary downturn, banks are more willing to pull the plug on smaller companies where loans are likely to be secured against assets.

As a company becomes more secure and builds a track record, it should be able to negotiate lower interest charges.

Pre-tax profit or loss

This is the line we are most interested in. Investors look for a return on their money and that will come from the payment of dividends, a rise in the share price or both. Neither will happen for long, if at all, where a company makes losses. Unfortunately, as we shall note in analysis later, a large proportion of smaller companies, especially those on AIM, do not make a profit.

In the main, we would naturally wish to invest in companies that not only make profits but also see those profits rise year by year.

It is admittedly possible to spot a loss-making company that has every prospect of becoming profitable soon. Losses may be falling sharply and new products may be coming to market. Shares in such companies are likely to be undervalued because investors have not yet spotted the potential. Good luck if you pick up this kind of bargain. Just be aware of the grave risk that those profits may never arrive.

Earnings per share

Earnings per share (EPS) are calculated by dividing post-tax profits by the number of shares in issue. As with profits, we would hope to see EPS increase year by year, or at least see any loss per share decreasing.

Growing companies often expand by buying other companies and, because they may not have cash to spare, will pay for those companies in shares rather than cash. The vendors of the companies taken over are likely to be content to take shares in a successful venture so they have a stake in the expected continued success of the enlarged group.

Creating new shares means those profits are being divided among more shareholders, potentially depressing EPS. It is therefore always worth checking whether EPS has risen in line with pre- and post-tax profits.

EBITDA

Companies that have not yet produced a pre-tax profit are fond of referring to earnings before interest, tax, depreciation and amortisation of assets, or EBITDA for short. EBITDA will always give a more favourable earnings figure than pre-tax profits simply because it includes all the earnings but excludes some of the costs.

Do not be lured by this siren. EBITDA is a highly dubious calculation that came into fashion for disguising losses during – you've guessed it – the dotcom boom when start-up companies found that real profits were hard to come by. How can one possibly justify excluding interest payments from any calculation of profits? Try telling that to the bank.

Five important things to check on an income statement

1. Does the company make a profit?

2. Are profits rising (or are losses coming to an end)?

3. Are sales improving?

4. Are costs under control?

5. Is there a dividend?

Case study: Asos

Let us look at a set of figures from online fashion retailer Asos, chosen because they present several interesting pointers in how to evaluate the performance of a company that has been adept at spotting opportunities. Asos was established in June 2000 and was originally called As Seen on Screen, selling its wares through a television channel. It joined AIM in

October the following year. It offers 6,500 fashion lines across womenswear, footwear, accessories, jewellery and beauty.

Do not be concerned that the figures have not been checked by an independent auditor. This is normal for interim figures and even full year figures, when first issued, are unaudited. They will be audited for inclusion in the annual report in due course.

Note also that these are *consolidated* (or group) *accounts*, which is what we want, rather than company accounts. In the case of small companies there is often just one operating company so this distinction will not matter. But if there is more than one company within a group, we want the consolidated accounts that lump everything together to give a full overview.

Unaudited consolidated income statement, six months ended 30 September 2007

	Unaudited 6 months to 30 September 2007	Unaudited 6 months to 30 September 2006
	£000s	£000s
Revenue	31,806	17,374
Cost of sales	(17,436)	(10,430)
Gross profit	14,370	6,944
Administrative expenses	(12,097)	(6,772)
Insurance proceed	-	570
Goodwill impairment	-	
Operating profit	2,273	742
Finance income	145	53
Profit before tax	2,418	795
Taxation	(745)	(233)
Profit after tax	1,673	562
Profit after tax on discontinued operations	-	45
Profit for the period	1,673	607
Earnings per Share		
Basic	2.3p	0.84p
Diluted	2.2p	0.80p

Analysis

The first thing to note is the top line, which shows a startling increase in revenue. While we would hope to invest in growing companies, we should check for the reason for any significant change. A sudden growth in revenue could arise from the acquisition of another company, in which case we would need to check whether there has been any genuine organic growth.

In the case of Asos, however, these were genuine sales increases. Asos had a clear strategy to compete in the tough fashion market by differentiating itself from High Street retailers such as Marks & Spencer and Monsoon. By specialising in designs similar to clothes worn by famous people, Asos found a niche fulfilling the aspirations of star gazers – and there are plenty of them, although the company prefers to call them internet savvy 16-35 year-olds.

There are two other potential problems with growing companies. The first is that future growth fails to live up to expectations so it is worth checking what the company statement says about current trading. On this occasion Asos was able to point to even faster growth, with sales doubling in the nine weeks between the half year end and the issuing of the figures, compared with 83% in the previous six months.

Victoria Beckham's dress sense may not be to everyone's taste but Asos had good reason to be grateful that the Spice Girl/soccer wife stayed in the public eye. One of the best selling new lines was a shift dress with a large bow based on a similar item worn by Posh Spice herself.

The second point to bear in mind is whether the company is becoming overstretched by too-rapid growth. It needs to be able to maintain supplies, handle the goods and the orders and get them to the customers. There was nothing to indicate that this was a problem at Asos but such difficulties tend to pop up unexpectedly, even at well run companies. For example, models maker Hornby was unable to meet a surge in demand in Europe, causing sales and profits to fall short.

Costs

The cost of sales line gives us an indication of whether costs are running out of control. In this case, while revenue was 83% higher, the cost of making or buying in the products was 67% higher. So gross profit margins had improved. While a leap in costs is normally a cause for concern, the key point is whether they are increasing more slowly than sales.

Similarly, administrative costs rose 79%, a very big increase but still lower than the improvement in sales.

One-off items

Always check whether odd items have distorted the profit figures. In this case, Asos benefited in the previous year from an insurance payment arising from factory damage caused by an explosion at the nearby fuel depot at Buncefield in 2005. Where such items occur, it is worth checking back through previous profit figures to see whether any of the current year's improvement is down to recovery from an earlier setback. On this occasion the bounceback occurred in the previous financial year, so none of the current sales boost was artificially inflated.

Goodwill impairment refers to any companies that may have been acquired in recent years. When an acquisition is made, goodwill is the amount paid on top of the value of the assets acquired. Accountancy rules require that this amount is written off in tranches each year until the figure is reduced to zero. The absence of any goodwill write-off in the Asos accounts indicates that its performance had not been flattered by taking over other companies. Growth had been entirely internal.

Where goodwill write-offs are made, pre-tax profits will be depressed until the figure is cleared. As this will not be directly relevant to the trading performance, it is best to consider this figure as an accounting anomaly and to disregard it in assessing how well a company is doing.

Profits

When the above calculations have been taken into account, the operating profit emerges. This is the profit that has been made in running the business. Naturally we hope that operating profits have risen year on year. Asos was able to report much improved figures thanks to sales outstripping costs.

Asos is then able to record that it received interest income from its spare cash, interest that has risen over the previous year as the cash pile has grown. Many companies will show this line in the accounts as a payment out as they incur interest on money borrowed to fund the business. A large interest payment out can indicate that the company is financially overstretched.

We can now arrive at the pre-tax profit, ultimately the most important figure on the accounts. We need to know whether a company makes a profit at all and whether the profits are rising or the loss is being reduced. In the final analysis, a loss making company will inevitably go under eventually while a company increasing its profits will have scope for paying increasing dividends.

We would hope to see a line in the accounts showing how much it has cost to pay any dividend. The absence of such a line indicates that Asos did not pay a dividend, which made it a less attractive investment for those seeking income. However, the existence of cash reserves was an indication that a dividend was possible in the future.

Earnings per share

Finally we have the earnings per share figure. This is calculated by dividing the after-tax profit by the number of ordinary shares in issue. It gives you a clear indication of how much profit the company has made for each share and this helps investors to calculate how much the shares are worth. We shall look more closely at this in the chapter on key ratios.

The basic earnings per share figure is based on the number of shares actually issued. The diluted figure is calculated on what the figure would have been if all share options had been taken up. This allows for any options granted to directors and also any convertible shares that could be swapped into ordinary shares.

The figure to go on is the basic calculation as this reflects the actual current situation.

Chart 8.1: ASOS

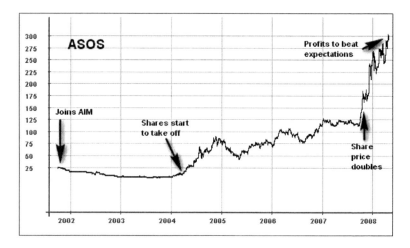

The positive signs in the income statement augured well for the future. ASOS chief executive Nick Robertson said in his next trading statement:

> We had a cracking Christmas. Sales were ahead of internal forecasts, margin remained strong and our stock position healthy. I can confirm that we experienced no major delivery issues in the run up to Christmas.

This was not a flash in the pan, for total sales for the 42 weeks to 20 January 2008 were 88% higher than in the same period a year earlier and Robertson was able to tell the stock market that pre-tax profits for the year to 31 March 2008 would be significantly ahead of expectations.

ASOS shares drifted along below 25p for more than two years before starting to take off early in 2004. They had a particularly good run up towards the end of 2007 as the stock market generally was flagging, more than doubling from 112.5p in mid-September to a peak of 266p at year end.

Key points:

- A company finding a niche market needs to be able to exploit it. Management needs to have an eye for the main chance.

- It is advantageous to be in a niche where fashions change or new processes are constantly being introduced so that it is possible to keep one step ahead of the opposition.

- While a niche player may stand still in terms of the size of the company, it should be always on the move in securing its future.

Case study: GW Pharmaceuticals

Let us contrast the ever improving story at Asos with the prolonged difficulties at GW Pharmaceuticals, which has been beset by many of the problems faced by smaller companies.

GW has struggled on with effectively just one product, and one that it has been prevented from selling. The product is Sativex, a cannabis-based drug intended primarily for relieving the symptoms of multiple sclerosis but which has also shown promising signs of easing the pain of cancer sufferers.

The pharmaceutical industry has been subject to enormous pressures over the past few years. The demand for new wonder drugs has opened up the field for research and development and there is a worldwide market for successful new discoveries.

However, testing drugs is an uncertain process. The overwhelming majority fail to come through a stringent series of tests and those that fail at the final hurdle will have incurred considerable costs.

While pharmaceutical companies naturally seek to recoup those costs by charging a premium price for their new drugs, health authorities are determined to hold down their own costs. Drugs have a comparatively short life protected by patents before they face competition from generic copies.

Finding a niche

In this trading climate, large pharmas have been happy to see smaller drug developers take the lead in finding new compounds and taking them through the first trials. The best prospects can then be supported through the later stages by the likes of Roche and Glaxo in return for marketing rights.

This scenario has attracted a number of small pharmaceuticals onto the stock market in what are high risk/high reward investments. The cash raised in floating the company will, it is hoped, see the company through to the stage where it starts to receive revenue.

Alas, this rarely, if ever, happens. Testing, from early experiments with animals through three phases of human trials, is so time consuming and expensive that a small company is unlikely to raise enough cash at one go to last right through to seeing the product on the chemists' shelves.

Sativex, made from cannabis grown by GW under strict security, was shown to produce significant improvements in a range of symptoms, including pain, muscle spasms, bladder problems and tremors as long ago as 2000-1, in some cases transforming lives, but GW has struggled to win approval in the UK from the Medical and Healthcare products Regulatory Agency (MHRA), the government body that decides whether to recommend drugs as being safe and effective.

The long delay caused by conducting more tests to satisfy MHRA has prevented GW from earning the revenue it expected, although a marketing deal with international pharmaceutical giant Bayer to sell Sativex in Canada and part of Spain has alleviated the situation.

Meanwhile the cost of growing cannabis, including high level security, processing the drug in expensive premises that conform to strict standards of sterility, testing them on increasing number of patients, processing data from the tests and making repeated submissions to health authorities here and abroad, has taken its inevitable toll.

These difficulties over several years are reflected in the following income statement:

Unaudited consolidated income statement, six months ended 31 March 2008

	Six months to 31 March 2008	Six months to 31 March 2007
	£000s	£000s
Revenue	5,695	823
Cost of sales	(136)	(85)
Gross profit	5,559	738
Research and development	(9,286)	(6,246)
Management and admin	(1,550)	(1,783)
Share-based payment	(372)	(666)
Operating loss	(5,649)	(7,957)
Interest income	464	393
Loss before tax	(5,185)	(7,564)
Tax credit	1,018	1,012
Loss for the period	(4,167)	(6,552)
Loss per share - basic and Diluted	(3.5p)	(5.5p)

Analysis

We can see from the revenue line that it has taken eight years from the start of tests for GW to start to receive any meaningful income. Nonetheless, we do have an indication that sales could grow rapidly if Sativex can be accepted in more countries.

Another positive side is that the cost of making these sales is comparatively small and has not risen sharply in line with increased sales. The cost of selling the product is borne by GW's larger international partners, so the gross profit, which is revenue minus the cost of sales, was also much improved.

The same cannot be said of research costs, however. It is always worth checking income statements for any items such as this that indicate special costs associated with the company's particular line of business.

Spending on management and administration has been kept commendably under control, an essential policy for a small company still waiting for income to rise to the point where it covers all costs.

The line on share-based payments is one that has become quite common on small, newer companies. Wage costs can be held down if staff are offered the incentive of free shares as part of their salaries. Accounting rules now demand that these appear as an item on the income statement, although they are not really a cost at all.

Losses

After all these costs have been taken into consideration, GW ran up another substantial operating loss, albeit a smaller one. There was still some cash in the bank, so GW recorded some income from interest payments, and the pre-tax loss meant that a tax credit could be carried over into a future financial year.

Start-up companies may amass tax credits over several years until they move into profit. These can then be offset against profits made until they are used up.

There is just one loss per share figure in each column. This is because those shares awarded as an incentive to staff have been issued. There are no options or warrants that can be turned into shares at a later date.

Chart 8.2: GW Pharma

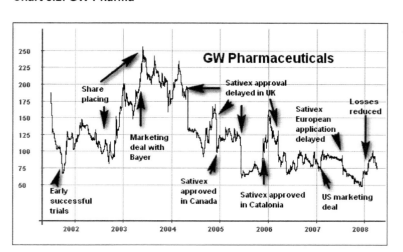

GW Pharmaceuticals shares have had a roller coaster ride, rising on hopes of approval in the UK and falling each time those hopes were dashed.

From around 190p in the middle of 2001 the shares fell back before soaring to a peak of 255p a year later on a wave of optimism that conveniently overlooked the realities of the situation. This was a remarkable performance at a time when the stock market generally was in the grip of a relentless bear market. Perhaps the desire for GW to succeed in bringing relief to sufferers of a crippling affliction such as MS clouded investors' judgment.

At all events, the shares went through several years of sharp falls on each disappointment followed by somewhat slower and ever weakening gains. Each peak in the share price was lower than the previous one, a classic sign of long term decline.

Finally they reached 50p at the end of 2007 before making another attempt to pick up again.

Key points

- Small pharmaceutical companies are risky investments, especially if they rely solely or mainly on one product. If that product fails to come through tests, or approval is delayed for any reason, then there is no revenue coming through and cash can run short.

- Small pharmas do not have political clout. They are heavily reliant on striking licensing deals with larger rivals.

- The scope for rewards if a product succeeds is enormous, with huge markets mainly in the US, Europe and Japan.

- Do not invest simply because you want to support a company that is searching for a worthwhile cure.

9.
Balance Sheet

Our main concern in looking at the balance sheet is to determine whether the company has sufficient financial resources to thrive. In this regard we should look at the figures in conjunction with the cash flow statement that is usually printed immediately after the balance sheet to determine whether the position is improving or giving cause for concern.

The balance sheet is an assessment of the company's assets (the things of value that it owns such as cash, property and machinery) and its liabilities (what the company owes, such as a bank overdraft and bills from suppliers).

As with the income statement, we can see from a comparison with previous years whether assets are growing faster than liabilities.

Fixed assets

The first line on the balance sheet will normally be fixed assets, items such as property and machinery owned and used by the business, that do not vary in value from day to day. These are calculated on the basis of original cost minus an amount written off to cover depreciation or, in the case of property, on the basis of an independent valuation.

Fixed assets may be broken down into tangibles and intangibles. The former are real solid assets while the latter is a vague notion of value such as *goodwill*. While tangibles can be used as security for borrowings, intangibles are of no real use if the company runs into financial difficulties.

Current assets and liabilities

Current means in the next 12 months. So cash at the bank and bills that customers are due to pay are current assets while bills from suppliers and bank loans due for repayment are current liabilities.

Assessing whether a company has net current assets (more is due to come in than to go out over the next 12 months) or net current liabilities (as things stand the company will be unable to pay all its bills) spells out the short term health of the company.

Net assets

When you deduct all liabilities from total assets you arrive at net assets. If this is a negative figure, that is the liabilities exceed the assets, then longer term financial difficulties are looming.

If a company is insolvent, which means it cannot continue trading without its problems becoming worse, the directors have a legal duty to cease trading.

Reserves

Profits built up over previous years, including any property revaluations, are shown as reserves. Dividends are paid from these reserves, so if losses rather than profits have been accumulated then by law no dividend can be paid. This is to prevent directors from paying to shareholders money that should rightfully go to creditors.

There will be no dividend until any such losses have been wiped out. This can be done either by accumulating sufficient profits from future trading to offset previous losses or by persuading a High Court judge that there is no danger of insolvency, in which case the company can be reconstructed to eliminate the deficit.

There will be other lines on the balance sheet, varying according to the line of business that the company is in, but we have concentrated on the ones that tell us the financial health of a potential investment.

Cash is king

The need for a sound cash position is important for companies of any size but they are of heightened interest in the case of small companies. Consider the following points.

- **Overdrafts**
  In times of trouble, the banks are extremely reluctant to pull the plug on a struggling large company because it would mean writing off hundreds of millions of pounds and the banks' own shareholders and the press would raise awkward questions over why such a large sum had been committed to a failing business. There is no such worry about

closing down a smaller company. Bad debts crop up all the time and one more small one will hardly attract headlines or opprobrium.

- **Secured loans**
  A larger company is more likely to have valuable assets to secure loans against. Secured loans incur lower interest rates and mean that the lender can allow the borrower greater leeway.

- **Interest rates**
  Small companies do not have the muscle power to negotiate better loan terms.

- **Start-up costs**
  New businesses incur costs in acquiring property, supplies, machinery, marketing and staff before they start to recoup the outlay through sales.

- **Share issues**
  A large company in need of a capital injection has a better chance of persuading existing and new shareholders to stump up cash because they have a wider spread of shareholders to appeal to. Institutional investors are more inclined to underwrite share issues by large companies while they do not want to be bothered with smaller, less lucrative issues by smaller companies.

Five important things to check on a balance sheet

1. Are assets greater than liabilities?
2. Are cash reserves sufficient to see the company through at least the next year?
3. Are there reserves to pay dividends out of?
4. Is cash flowing in or out?
5. Are debts proportionate to the size of the company and are they rising or falling?

With these issues in mind, let us look at the balance sheets and cash flow tables that accompanied the income statements we examined in the previous chapter.

We will look again at Asos.

Case study: ASOS

Unaudited consolidated (condensed) balance sheet, 30 September 2007

	Unaudited 30 September 2007	Unaudited 30 September 2006	Audited 31 March 2007
	£000s	£000s	£000s
Non current assets			
Goodwill	1,060	1,248	1,060
Property, plant and equipment	2,974	1,687	2,086
Deferred tax asset	560	411	490
	4,594	3,346	3,636
Current assets			
Inventories	8,231	5,202	5,683
Trade and other receivables	2,791	1,926	1,669
Cash and cash equivalents	5,857	1,160	5,379
	16,879	8,288	12,731
Current liabilities	(11,834)	(5,453)	(7,982)
Net current assets	5,045	2,835	4,749
Net assets	9,639	6,181	8,385
Called up share capital	2,548	2,520	2,544
Share premium	3,185	3,259	3,128
EBT own shares	(943)	-	(236)
Retained earnings	4,849	402	2,949
Total shareholders' funds	9,639	6,181	8,385

Unaudited consolidated (condensed) cash flow statement for the six months ended 30 September 2007

	Unaudited 6 months to 30 September 2007	Unaudited 6 months to 30 September 2006	Audited 12 months to 31 March 2007
	£000s	£000s	£000s
Cash generated from operations	2,344	(1,923)	3,116
Net cash from returns on investment and servicing of finance	145	53	124
Net cash outflow from investing activities	(1,301)	(887)	(1,578)
Net cash (outflow)/inflow from financing activities	(647)	28	(87)
Net (decrease)/increase in cash from discontinued operations	(63)	146	60
Net Increase/(decrease) in cash and cash equivalents	478	(2,583)	1,635

Analysis

We are not too concerned about non-current assets. While these might, at a push, raise cash for shareholders if the company folded or shut up shop of its own volition, we are naturally looking to invest in going concerns with a healthy future.

We are interested in current assets, which are cash or items that will be turned into cash in the next 12 months, and current liabilities, effectively bills that will have to be met within the same time frame. In other words, we are looking to see if there are any imminent dangers and whether the position is improving or deteriorating.

In the case of Asos we can see that current assets have increased over the past 12 months and over the past six months and the comfort zone by which they exceed current liabilities is widening. This improvement is shown in the line for net current assets, which is current assets minus current liabilities.

We might be a little concerned about the sharp rise in inventory levels over the past six months given the trend over several years for retailers to reduce the amount of unsold stock they carry, partly because it soaks up working capital and partly because unsold stock has to be cleared at heavily reduced prices when it gets out of date. However, with Asos we know from the income statement that sales are rising rapidly so an increase in stock levels to meet demand is quite acceptable, indeed desirable.

Similarly one would want to know why trade and other receivables, the money that Asos is owed by its customers, is rising. Again, this is perfectly reasonable given the rise in sales.

We are further reassured by the cash flow statement. Retailers generally do better over the Christmas period, which falls in the second half of the Asos financial year, and it is most encouraging to see a healthy inflow of cash in the first half covered, a big improvement on the previous first half. This has allowed Asos to step up the investment of cash in the business.

The position at GW Pharmaceuticals reflects the rather different set of circumstances there.

Case study: GW Pharmaceuticals

Unaudited consolidated balance sheet, 31 March 2008

	31 March 2008	31 March 2007	30 September 2007
	£000s	£000s	£000s
Non-current assets			
Intangible assets - goodwill	5,210	5,210	5,210
Property, plant & equipment	1,183	1,044	1,082
	6,393	**6,254**	**6,292**
Current assets			
Inventories	608	665	535
Trade and other receivables	1,935	4,940	2,815
Cash and cash equivalents	18,488	21,914	20,966
	21,031	**27,519**	**24,316**
Total assets	27,424	33,773	30,608
Current liabilities			
Trade and other payables	(9,180)	(6,286)	(7,634)
Net current assets	**11,851**	**21,233**	**16,682**
Non-current liabilities			
Deferred revenue	(16,349)	(18,249)	(17,299)
Long-term provisions	(20)	(54)	(12)
Total liabilities	(25,549)	(24,589)	(24,945)
Net assets	**1,875**	**9,184**	**5,663**
Equity			
Share capital	120	120	120
Share premium account	58,279	58,223	58,272
Other reserves	19,262	19,262	19,262
Retained earnings	(75,786)	(68,421)	(71,991)
Total equity	**1,875**	**9,184**	**5,663**

GW Pharmaceuticals plc
Consolidated cash flow statement - Unaudited for the six months ended 31 March 2008

	Six months to 31 March 2008	Six months to 31 March 2007	Year ended 30 September 2007
	£000s	£000s	£000s
Net cash from operating activities	(2,620)	1,950	569
Investing activities			
Interest received	443	357	960
Purchases of property, plant and equipment	(308)	(281)	(500)
Net cash from investing activities	135	76	460
Financing activities			
Proceeds on issue of shares	7	13	62
Net (decrease)/increase in cash and cash equivalents	(2,478)	2,039	1,091
Cash and cash equivalents at beginning of year	20,966	19,875	19,875
Cash and cash equivalents at end of the period	18,488	21,914	20,966

Analysis

With inventories little changed, while receivables and the cash pile dwindled, current assets have been sliding. Current liabilities have, in contrast, increased, leading to a fall in net current assets at a rate that raises cause for serious concern.

Note also the line on retained earnings, bearing in mind that a number in brackets is a negative figure. At this point GW had run up accumulated pre-tax losses of £75.8m over the years, a sobering thought for a small company.

The cash flow statement, unsurprisingly, shows an outflow of cash. However, one point of reassurance is that there is sufficient cash to last for several years at the current rate of outflow. There is therefore some hope that, if it can obtain more markets for its products, it can survive until it turns the corner.

Key points

- Having sufficient cash reserves is even more important for smaller companies than large ones.

- Smaller companies are more vulnerable to the withdrawal of support from banks or from business failures among its customers.

10.

Fundamentals

Although we can find information on smaller companies, including their financial figures, assessing whether we should make a particular investment often presents problems.

As with larger companies, we would normally look specifically at two key ratios:

1. price/earnings ratio

2. dividend yield

We want to see how the stock market rates our proposed investment in comparison with: the market as a whole, with other smaller company shares and with the sector in which the company is classified.

Price earnings ratio

Our first stumbling block is that many small companies do not make a post-tax profit on which earnings per share can be calculated. No earnings means that we cannot calculate an historic PE. While it is possible that there is a broker forecast on which we can base a prospective PE, this is unlikely unless the company is expected to move into profit, and even then there will probably be research only from the house broker.

At any given time more than half the companies outside the FTSE 350 index will have failed to show a profit in the past financial year. It is not possible to give a precise percentage because the numbers will fluctuate as each new set of results is published but fewer Small Caps make profits than midcaps, and fewer Fledglings make profits than Small Caps, while AIM stocks have by far the poorest profits record. The profits table (below) for 2007 is typical.

Table: Number of small companies making a profit (2007)

Index	Companies in index	Companies making a profit
Small Cap	294	253 (86%)
Fledgling	219	157 (72%)
AIM	2,229	638 (29%)

The preceding table shows the numbers of companies making a profit in the three small company indices: FTSE Small Cap, FTSE Fledgling, and FTSE AIM. As can be seen the range is wide: 86% of companies in the Small Cap index make a profit, whereas only 29% of AIM companies do.

Sources for PE data

The most extensive newspaper list of company share price data is contained in the *Financial Times*. There is no need to buy it every day as PE ratios will not normally change dramatically from day to day unless stock markets are particularly volatile. The ratio will change, though, when a company produces new profit figures or issues a trading statement that prompts analysts to revise their earnings forecasts, as for example in the case of a profit warning.

Reasonably full, though less comprehensive, tables appear in *The Times*, *Daily Telegraph* and *The Independent*. Those in the *Daily Mail* may be helpful but the list is too short to cover many smaller companies.

PE ratios can also be found on most financial data websites such as Yahoo, ADVFN, Reuters and Citywire.

The actual figures given by the various sources can differ according to how they are calculated. The main difference is between historic figures based on the most recent full-year results and prospective figures based on analysts' forecasts for the current and following years.

Prospective figures will depend on how many forecasts the compiler has access to; although in the case of the smallest companies the calculation should not vary widely for the simple reason that there will be only one or two analysts covering the company. In many cases only the house broker will provide a forecast.

PE analysis

It is not possible to state what a reasonable PE is for many reasons. Much depends on whether investors are optimistic or pessimistic about the economy and the future performance of UK shares. In times of economic growth, when investors believe earnings will rise, PEs also rise in anticipation of better times ahead. When the outlook is uncertain, PEs will fall to allow for possible future disappointment.

Historically, the UK stock market as a whole has had an average PE of 13 or 14. This figure is calculated from the PEs of companies in the All-Share index. In times of exuberance and optimism the figure can creep up towards 20, though the UK market never reaches the ludicrous heights of Asian markets where PEs can climb to triple figures. It would take a really gloomy prognosis on the economy to push the market average down to single figures although this can happen to individual sectors, as evidenced by house builders during the credit crunch. The sector average fell to as low as seven times prospective earnings while the average for the market as a whole was 11.

However, we would expect a lower figure for all but the more solidly established smaller companies because of the greater investment risk.

PEs also vary from sector to sector. A sector may be out of favour because prospects have taken a tumble, as happened with finance and housebuilding during the credit crunch. Sectors with strong growth prospects, such as technology stocks, will tend to have higher PEs while solid but pedestrian sectors, such as basic manufacturing, will have lower PEs.

To get a fair perspective of the stock market's view on any prospective investment it is important to compare the company with its peers.

The PE should always be considered alongside the income statement and the balance sheet, whatever the size of the company, but this is especially important in the case of smaller companies that offer, on the whole, greater risks and greater potential rewards.

Even where a company has no historic PE we should not necessarily reject the possibility of making an investment, although we should be very careful before doing so. The income statement and other information on the company will give us some idea of whether there is any reasonable prospect of a profit in the near future.

What the PE tells us

Where a company's PE is out of line with the stock market average – or, more importantly, with those for other companies in the same sector – we should investigate why. A high PE indicates that the market believes the company has great prospects. Companies such as Speedy Hire and Domino's Pizza had high PEs as small companies because investors believed that they would continue to grow strongly and that increased earnings would compensate for the high ratio.

On the other hand a low PE could highlight an opportunity crying out to be spotted, an undervalued company that is still below the radar of institutional investors but which will eventually be appreciated, and will pay decent dividends until it is.

Alas, there is no magic formula that tells you whether to buy. The market could be wrong in overvaluing a company with a high PE. Perhaps it will be overstretched as it grows too quickly. Or perhaps the market is right to assign a lowly valuation because some new adverse factor is emerging such as its sales coming under pressure from new competitors.

No one gets it right all the time, not even the professional investors.

Dividend yield

The other key ratio, the dividend yield – usually referred to simply as the yield – raises similar issues to the price/earnings ratio, only more so. The yield is calculated by dividing the dividend per share by the share price. Note that if there is no dividend, the yield is zero.

The proportion of small companies paying a dividend is even smaller than the number making a profit.

Table: Number of small companies paying a dividend (2007)

Index	Companies in index	Companies paying a dividend
Small Cap	294	250 (85%)
Fledgling	219	129 (59%)
AIM	2,229	342 (15%)

As we saw in the previous section on PEs, there is a big difference between the indices on the proportion of companies that pay dividends. 85% of companies in the FTSE Small Cap pay dividends, while only 15% of AIM companies do.

It is rare for a loss-making company to pay a dividend, since the payment has to be funded out of reserves which will be rapidly depleted. In addition, companies making small profits and those that have made losses in the past are likely to preserve cash to keep the business going rather than return it to shareholders.

Once again, we need to check back to the financial statements. If a company does not pay a dividend, we can ask whether it is likely to do so soon by asking these questions:

1. Is it making increasing profits, or at least reducing its losses to the point where a profit is imminent?

2. Does it have retained earnings, built up from previous years' profits, or retained losses? Any accumulated losses will have to be eliminated, either by making profits or gaining High Court approval to write them off, before a dividend can legally be paid.

3. Does it have cash balances and a positive cash flow so there is money to pay a dividend with?

Dividend cover

If the company does pay a dividend it is worth checking the *dividend cover* – that is the extent to which dividends per share are covered by earnings per share.

The norm for large companies is that earnings should cover dividends twice over, so that for every pound paid in dividends the company retains one pound to reinvest in the business. This is not a hard and fast rule and certainly not a legal requirement. Some companies are more circumspect than others and companies may let the ratio fall in hard times rather than reduce the dividend in line with earnings.

We would expect smaller companies to maintain a higher dividend cover than larger ones because:

- Directors may prefer to reduce bank borrowings that have been incurred during the start-up years

- They may take a cautious view of prospects if the company has not had a long trading history

- They may be concerned that profits will come under pressure from larger competitors

- They may prefer to amass a cash pile as a safety precaution

Interest cover

One other important calculation we should bear in mind is how comfortably the company is able to meet any interest payments it has to make. *Interest cover* is calculated by dividing pre-tax profits by the net interest payment. The more times interest is covered, the less problematic it is.

Again, there is no specific figure that applies to all companies but we would expect a larger company to cover interest payments at least five times so smaller companies should prudently provide interest cover of six times or more. However, we should not be dogmatic about this figure.

Start-up companies are likely to have borrowed to get going until revenue from sales starts to roll in. We must use our judgment to decide if there is a good reason for lower interest cover and whether the cover is likely to grow within the next 12 months.

One exception is where new companies have borrowed from their own directors rather than from the bank. Here the ratio can be much lower, although we would raise an eyebrow if interest cover falls towards one – ie profits only just cover the interest due. Directors are much less willing to pull the plug than the banks are.

11.

Liquidity

There are plenty of highly liquid small companies on the main board and on AIM. However, there are also many smaller companies which might be difficult to trade because of their poor liquidity (ie, they have low trading volumes). This is not an insuperable problem but you should be aware of it when making your investment decisions.

Trading volumes

The following table shows the average daily trading volume (in shares) and the average daily turnover for five FTSE indices.

Table: Comparative trading volumes and turnover (August 2008)

Index	Avg Daily Volume	Avg Daily Turnover (£)
FTSE 100	15,463,410	72,084,461
FTSE 250	2,177,030	5,351,156
FTSE Small Cap	292,710	263,683
FTSE Fledgling	69,043	25,096
FTSE AIM	196,965	74,356

The average daily volume was the average of 20 trading days in August 2008. The average daily turnover was calculated by multiplying the average daily volume with the share price at the end of the 20-day period. The figures are obviously subject to fluctuation – both volumes and price can change dramatically for individual shares from one day to the next.

Although the individual figures may fluctuate, the table gives a useful rough measure of the comparative liquidity of large and small companies.

For example, the average daily trading volume of FTSE 250 companies is just over 2 million shares; while their average daily turnover is £5.3m. In other words, for most FTSE 250 companies there should not be much trouble buying or selling £20,000 worth of shares in one trade.

By contrast, the average daily trading volume of FTSE Fledgling companies is only about 69,000 shares, while their average daily turnover is £25,000. Therefore, trying to buy or sell £20,000 of shares in one trade could be tricky – as this is almost the average turnover for the whole day.

From the above table it might appear that AIM stocks have better liquidity than Fledgling stocks. But this is not necessarily so: the AIM figures are heavily influenced by the few large companies that trade on AIM. Over half the companies trading on AIM have turnover of less than £2,000 on an average day.

While larger companies have hundreds of millions, even billions, of shares in issue, smaller companies may have only a few hundred thousand shares up for grabs, especially if a large stake is still in the hands of the founders or a financial institution that provided support in the early days.

It will be difficult to buy shares, certainly in large numbers and, more importantly, it will be difficult to sell them when you decide to take your profits or cut your losses.

Attempts to improve liquidity

The LSE has, to its credit, made valiant efforts to maintain and improve liquidity at the smaller end of the market. That was the motivation behind the establishment of AIM, which replaced the moribund and illiquid Unlisted Securities Market. It is also why different trading systems have been set up to tailor a suitable method of buying and selling shares to the needs of different sizes of companies.

The exchange has launched a further consultation on other measures aimed at boosting liquidity in the shares of smaller companies. It will be consulting member firms on measures it could take to improve the setting of share prices and the provision of liquidity for smaller companies. Under consideration are changes to market making obligations, the costs associated with market maker registration and the reduction, and possible removal of reporting fees in less liquid equities on the main market and AIM.

Normal market size

To help investors, the LSE has allotted a normal market size to each quoted company. This is usually referred to as the NMS but it is sometimes also called the exchange market size. It defines what is a reasonable sized trade for each company and, for companies traded on SEAQ and SEATS, indicates the size of order that a market maker will be prepared to handle.

The larger the NMS, the more liquid a company's shares are. Before investing in any company's shares, you can check its NMS on the LSE's website www.londonstockexchange.com by going into the Investor Centre and selecting Company Profile in the Tools column. Click on Free Company Profile. If you want to read the profile on screen rather than have it emailed to you, don't fill in your email address.

Here is a sample of companies mentioned in this book and the NMS for each.

Table: sample of NMS values for selected companies

Company	Trading system	Market	NMS
GW Pharmaceuticals	SETS	AIM	1,250
Speedy Hire	SETS	Main	750
Asos	SETS	AIM	5,000
Woolworths	SETS	Main	50,000
Theo Fennell	SEAQ	AIM	500
Manpower Software	SEAQ	AIM	1,000

We would, on the whole, expect larger companies to have a larger NMS but we can see from the table that this is not necessarily the case. Woolworths has seen its share price and its market capitalisation collapse but it still has an NMS several times greater than that of Speedy Hire, which has grown dramatically in size through expansion and acquisitions. We can also note that the NMS of a company on AIM is not necessarily smaller than that for a company with a full listing.

NMS can depend not only on the number of shares in issue but also factors such as whether large stakes are in a few hands and whether existing shareholders hang on to their holdings.

As the NMS is the normal size of order that the market can handle easily, it is the largest number of shares that you are likely to be able to deal in at one go. In effect, the NMS is the number of shares that can change hands without dramatically affecting the share price.

This is a point to bear in mind if you are tempted to build a sizeable stake in a company with a small NMS. When you buy you will probably have to do so in several batches. Similarly, when you decide to cash in your investment it is possible, indeed likely, that you will be unable to sell a large batch of shares in one go.

This can have an adverse impact on ability to buy and sell at the price you want. Each purchase you make will help to push the price higher and each sale will push it lower.

Say you wish to buy 5,000 shares in Theo Fennell. You are likely to get the first 500 shares at the prevailing market offer price, but then the market maker might raise its quoted buy and sell prices to attract a seller to counterbalance your purchase. You may be able to find another market maker to sell you the second batch of 500 shares but after that the price will move further and further against you as the supply of sellers dries up. Furthermore, the market makers will widen the spread between their buy and sell prices in an attempt to rebalance their books.

This is even more important for those investors who like to run stop-loss positions. When a share price falls heavily it may be impossible to sell all your shares at the price you have set and it may be impossible to get even a small batch away at your stop-loss price. When confidence in a small company collapses, so does the share price because there will be few, if any, buyers speculating on recovery.

The spread

The less liquid a particular share is, the wider the spread between the buying and selling price is likely to be.

For example, at the time of writing you could buy shares in retailer Marks & Spencer, one of the largest and most liquid stocks on the London Stock Exchange, for 224.75p each or sell them at 224.5p. The spread is the difference between the buying and selling which in this case was only 0.25p or 0.1%.

The price you buy at is normally referred to as the offer price, that is the price at which the shares are on offer. The price at which you can sell is the bid price, the price at which the broker is bidding for your shares.

At the same time, models maker Hornby had a spread of 2.5p between its offer price of 144.5p and its bid price of 142p. This gap was 1.7%, which meant that anyone buying would need to see the shares move up 1.7% just to break even.

Spreads are not fixed. Different companies have different spreads and the spreads for individual companies can change throughout a day's trading.

This is usually not much of a problem with shares traded on SETS, whatever the size of the company, because this trading board is where the most readily available stocks change hands. As mentioned before, the system automatically matches up buyers and sellers. The gap between what the highest bidder is prepared to pay and the lowest price any seller will accept is unlikely to be more than a couple of pence and frequently during the course of each trading day the spread will gradually narrow until a deal is struck somewhere in the middle.

However, it is on SEAQ that the majority of smaller companies are traded. These are the stocks that rely on market makers to set buy and sell prices and the market makers will wish to maintain a sufficient spread to recompense themselves for providing this service. They buy at the lower price and sell at the higher price, making a small profit on each deal.

Unlike SETS, it is quite likely that SEAQ stocks will have a spread of 2p and the gap can widen if trading in a particular stock is volatile, say after a profit warning or unexpectedly good results.

All SEAQ stocks have at least two market makers so there is some competition that helps to narrow the spread. If one market maker is short of stock and sets a higher buying price, it is likely that another market maker will be prepared to deal at a lower price.

The position is less favourable for investors in those shares traded on SEATS Plus. Here you are at the mercy of just one market maker or, worse still, your broker may have to match your buy order up with a sell order from another investor.

The effect of the spread

Let us look at a range of companies and their spreads on the same day around 11am (one of the busiest trading times on the London stock market). All the companies in the table feature in this book except for Marks & Spencer, which is included as an example of a FTSE 100 company.

Half the companies chosen are traded on SETS and the other half on SEAQ.

Company	Index	Platform	Bid price	Offer price	Spread	%	Value of £1,000
Marks & Spencer	100	SETS	224.5p	224.75p	0.25p	0.1%	£968.89
Domino's Pizza	250	SETS	178.5p	178.75	0.25p	0.1%	£968.60
Hornby	SC	SETS	142p	144.5p	2.5p	1.7%	£952.70
Regent Inns	FL	SETS	3.7p	3.99p	0.29p	7.3%	£897.32
Clipper Wind	AIM	SEAQ	528p	535p	7p	1.3%	£956.92
Cluff Gold	AIM	SEAQ	70p	71.5p	1.5p	2.1%	£949.02
Theo Fennell	AIM	SEAQ	31p	34p	3p	8.8%	£981.76
Pan Andean	AIM	SEAQ	11.5p	13p	1.5p	11.5%	£854.62

Spreads are normally referred to as the number of pence between the bid and offer prices. However, this can be misleading as what really matters to investors is the percentage difference.

Clipper Windpower appears to have the largest spread at 7p but this has to be seen in the context of its higher share price. In reality, its spread is narrower at 1.3% than five other companies in our table.

In contrast, Regent Inns has a spread of only 0.29p, little wider than Marks & Spencer, yet this is a substantial gap for a share trading at less than 4p. In percentage terms, Regent's spread is one of the widest.

We can see that, on the whole, spreads on shares traded on SETS were narrower than on SEAQ but this was not always the case. Regent Inns had been through a period of sharp decline and although it had been included on SETS in its halcyon days its shares were no longer heavily traded.

In contrast to this anachronism, Clipper Windpower on SEAQ had a smaller spread in percentage terms than either Hornby or Regent Inns.

The effect of the spread can be seen in the final column. Assuming you bought £1,000 worth of shares in each company, paying £12.50 for each trade plus 0.5% stamp duty, then resold them immediately, again incurring broker's fees of £12.50 each trade, this is the amount of money you would get back.

In the case of Domino's Pizza, we would need the bid price to move up fairly modestly to 184.25p to recover our £1,000.

Pan Andean would have to hit 13.5p. That represents a gain of more than 17% – just to make nothing. Regent Inns would have to rise over 11% to allow us to recover our investment.

Clearly, the more actively you trade, the more ground you have to make up. If you traded in and out of Pan Andean four times over a few days when the share price didn't move at all, you would lose over half of your investment – eaten up by the spread and costs.

Holding onto a share for a couple of years gives adequate time for your chosen company to recover lost ground. Buying a share in the hope of turning in a profit within a few days is somewhat daunting.

Penny stocks

It is especially important to take the spread into account when buying penny stocks. Remember that the price quoted in the newspapers is, in the case of less liquid stocks, the middle price halfway between the buying and selling prices.

Say a share has a mid-price of 3p. It may seem quite easy to double your money if the company comes good. After all, a rise of just 3p will do while a share costing 100p has to move up another 100p to double in value.

Appearances are deceptive. The buying price could be 4p and the selling price may be 2p. So the selling price has to double for you just to break even (and that is without taking the stockbroker's charges and stamp duty into account).

Let us take an extreme example to drive home the point. Chemicals group Hardide was, at the time of writing, trading at 1.75p, with a bid price of 1.5p and an offer price of 2p.

So 10,000 shares would cost you £200 plus £12.50 broker's fee plus £1 stamp duty, a total of £213.50. You might well have to pay the broker more unless you are dealing online.

To recover your outlay you would need the offer price to rise to around 2.25p. That would give you a return of £225 minus £12.50 broker's fee, leaving you with £212.50. The bid price has gone up 50% yet you have still lost £1 on the investment!

Points to remember

- You may not be able to buy as many shares as you would like or you may have difficulty in dealing at the price you think is fair. Similarly you face the corresponding difficulty of finding a buyer when you want to sell.

- It is important to stipulate to your broker the price at which you want to buy and sell shares in smaller companies and to be prepared to tweak the price if there are no takers.

- It is possible to tell your broker to deal at 'best price' – in other words you accept the best deal available in the market at the moment you trade. This is not too risky with liquid stocks where the spread is tighter but you can find yourself paying significantly more, or selling for substantially less, than you intended with less liquid stocks.

- Never trade at best price in the first hour that the stock market is open in the morning except in a dire emergency. Spreads even in liquid stocks tend to be widest then as potential buyers and sellers move cautiously until they see how the land lies.

12.

What Drives Share Prices

Factors that drive share prices are common to companies of all sizes but the effects of each criterion may be greater or lesser in the case of smaller companies:

* stock market sentiment

* company announcements

* rumours

* share tips

* director's deals

* active investors

Let us look at each factor in turn.

Market sentiment

Surprisingly, it is the smaller companies that initially drive changes to the way that the whole market is moving. One would expect the largest companies to lead the way up or down, depending on whether we are in a bull or a bear market, yet it is the tiddlers who swim in the vanguard.

Two recent key moments in stock market history illustrate the point.

At the end of the severe bear market, which lasted from the start of the millennium to March 2003, it was smaller companies that raced higher through the summer months. The FTSE 100 lumbered along for several months until nervous investors were finally convinced that the bear market was over.

However, once the FTSE 100 gathered momentum in 2004 and 2005, the small caps and AIM stocks waited for the big boys to catch up.

Char 12.1: FTSE Small Cap v FTSE 100 (2003-2007)

Chart 12.2: FTSE AIM v FTSE 100 (2003-2007)

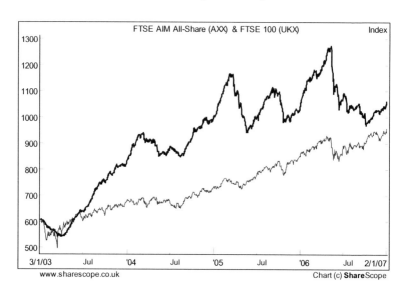

Similarly, the clouds that became the credit crunch started to gather right at the beginning of 2007 with defaults on US home loans. This all seemed a long way from the day-to-day doings of our smallest companies, but yet again the small cap and AIM indices reacted more quickly while the FTSE peaked in August that year. It was not until January 2008, when the FTSE slumped 14% in one month, that the biggest companies felt the most pain.

Chart 12.3: FTSE Small Cap v FTSE 100 (2007-2008)

Company announcements

Shares in all companies of every size are naturally affected by company announcements but you often have to be more patient with smaller companies as favourable results go unnoticed by larger investors. Don't worry. As we shall see in the chapter on upwardly mobile companies, the market will cotton on to quality in due course.

Profit warnings tend to have an immediate impact and a more dramatic one than in the case of larger companies because there is a greater danger that a small company will be unable to trade through a difficult period.

Rumours

Rumours are the stuff that stock markets are made of. Some prove to be accurate because inevitably word of impending takeovers and profit crashes leak out. But also tales are put around simply to manipulate the share price so that the people who start or circulate them can buy at depressed prices or sell at inflated ones.

Newspapers tend to concentrate on rumours concerning the larger companies, although stock market reports cover sharp movements in the price of smaller companies where these have been prompted by a rumour.

That gives free rein to bulletin boards on financial websites, where rumours concerning smaller companies abound. Such postings should be treated with extreme scepticism. Most bulletin board users hide behind pseudonyms as bizarre as the stories they propagate. These pseudonyms can be discarded readily if they become discredited when wild rumours prove unfounded.

There is a stock market saying that where there's a tip there's a tap. In other words, people put round tips and rumours for their own benefit, not for the general wellbeing of the investment community. In the case of smaller companies with fewer shares and little share trading, share prices can be moved substantially if a rumour prompts just a handful of deals.

Rumours can prove to be true. Just think carefully before you believe them. On the whole it is better to miss an opportunity to make a killing than to rush in and find that you are the victim.

Share tips

The difficulty of liquidity is a factor to be borne in mind when you consider whether to follow a tip issued by a broker or a newspaper. The big drawback of these tips is that they are usually based on results announced the previous day. This is particularly so in the case of newspaper columns unless there is such a dearth of company announcements that financial journalists are forced to use their own initiative and find their own stories to write. Analysts, to be fair, are more inclined to review companies when there is no news but even they have to write when there is something to say.

This news has been released through the stock market the previous day, most of it at 7am, so the market has had a whole day's trading to react. Given that share prices for smaller, less liquid companies tend to shoot up or down more sharply on news than those of larger ones, it is likely that the best investment opportunity will have gone, for the moment at least, long before you see the newspaper comment.

The best strategy in these situations is, firstly, to consider whether the market has in fact failed to react fully to the news or, alternatively, has over-reacted. That means there is still some scope for an investment.

Secondly, where there is a sound investment case for buying a company's shares, but the price has been pushed too high, look to see if the share price falls back when the euphoria of the results has died down. There may be a second chance to buy at a sensible price some days or even weeks later.

It is generally not a sound idea to chase the shares higher in these circumstances in a desperate rush to get on board. The shares are unlikely to rise further until there is more good news to push them higher. It could be a long wait.

Accept that the chance has been missed and look for opportunities elsewhere.

Directors' deals

Share purchases and sales by directors can be a barometer of how well a company of any size is doing. They know the business and its prospects better than anyone – or they certainly should do given their day-to-day involvement.

Such deals are a particularly important guide for other investors but extra caution is required in the case of smaller companies. While a purchase or sale of a small batch of shares will have little effect on a company with a stock market capitalisation of tens of billions of pounds, it can have a dramatic impact on the share price of a small company whose shares are only thinly traded.

So if a share price moves sharply higher after a director buys, it may be worth waiting to see if the price falls back rather than rushing in at a higher level.

A director with a majority or very large stake may take the opportunity of a buoyant share price to spread the holding more evenly so there is greater liquidity in the shares. If a major shareholder places shares with institutions that can be a good sign that new investors want to come in.

On the other hand, if a director with substantial holdings reduces his or her stake considerably for no apparent reason, one should wonder why. It could be a sign of lack of confidence in the company.

Share purchases by a director, while usually a good sign, should also be queried. Such purchases may be a desperate attempt to shore up a depressed share price. This is especially important if a dominant director is adding to an existing majority holding, putting the company even further under his or her control. The shares will never be liquid until this stake is unravelled, so the last thing you want is for the shares to be increasingly within one person's ownership.

Special care should be taken to check if any share dealing is the result of exercising share options. Executives of all sizes of companies are often awarded new shares free or at a reduced price as an incentive to drive up the share price.

This is often true of small start-up companies where there are greater risks of failure and the directors expect commensurate rewards if all goes well. It is quite common for executives to immediately sell their bonus shares in the market.

Case study: PayPoint

The two top directors at electronic payment services group PayPoint sold over 600,000 shares in February 2008, raising well over £3m between them.

PayPoint specialises in processing electronic payments, mainly in the UK and Ireland. Its services are used by convenience grocery chains including the Co-op, Spar, Sainsbury Local and independents.

Apart from growing through increasing its existing business, it expanded through acquisitions in 2007, moving into Romania by buying mobile top-up supplier PayStore and establishing an online payments arm with the purchase of SecPay.

This policy of reasonably modest expansion in areas where the group had expertise produced a period of strong trading. In the four months to February 2008, the number of PayPoint terminal sites increased by 3.3% to 23,380 while those in the less developed market of Romania jumped 8.1% to 3,899.

The group was thus able to issue a strong trading statement and chairman David Newlands and chief executive Dominic Taylor took the opportunity provided by the news being out in the open to sell shares at 600p apiece.

Newlands parted with 290,000 shares for more than £1.7m while Taylor sold about 330,000, including some held on his behalf in a trust, pocketing nearly £2m in the process.

Newlands reduced his stake to just over 5,000 shares, which means he parted with 98% of his existing holding. On the other hand, Taylor retained just over 1.2m shares in a trust.

Chart 12.4: PayPoint

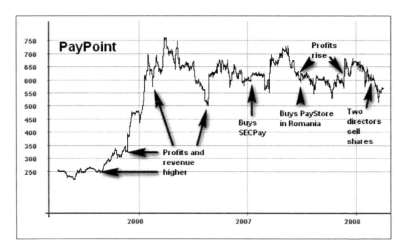

Interestingly, they did not pick the best time to sell. Ahead of the trading statement, PayPoint shares had been up to 650p and towards the end of 2007 they hit 660p. On the other hand, they avoided the worst of the recent performance: the shares dropped below 580p in December 2007 and they fell all the way to 516p within five weeks of the directors' sales.

Lessons to be learnt

- Directors cannot always pick the best time to buy or sell shares.

- In the case of sales, check whether the directors who are selling are retaining a substantial stake as a mark of confidence in the company. If more than one director sells at the same time it can be a worrying sign.

Case study: Norcros

When a profit warning in February 2008 sent the shares crashing 20%, two Norcros directors showed faith in the company by buying shares.

Norcros, which makes tiles and showers, said consumer uncertainty in the UK and power supply problems in South Africa would cause it to marginally miss forecasts for the year to 31 September, 2008. However, the company said that profits would still beat those for the previous 12 months: it was just that the improvement would fall short of previous expectations.

Chief executive Joe Matthews and company secretary David Hamilton both took advantage of the temporary share price fall to top up their holdings, paying 42p a share.

Matthews bought 200,000 shares to raise his stake to 2.25m, 1.75% of the company, while Hamilton picked up 400,000 through his self-invested pension plan. He now had ownership of nearly 1.5m Norcros shares, 1.15%.

Chart 12.5: Norcros

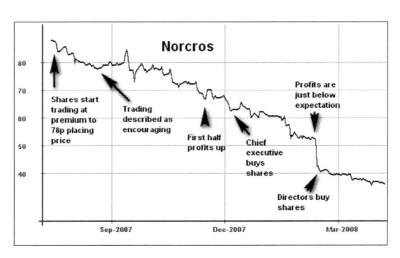

The brave act of defiance did not halt the slide in the shares, though. By the end of March they had slipped to 37p.

In mid April Norcros issued a trading update suggesting that revenue was up 5% year-on-year but it did not expect its markets to improve in the short term. By this stage the shares were down to 30p.

Key points

- Watch for directors buying shares after disappointing news. It can be a sign that things are not as bad as they seem on the surface.

Active investors

If you are looking for a bit of excitement and have a happy habit of being able to shut off your brain at night and sleep soundly, then you will welcome the attention of active investors, a group of mysterious sounding people who are on the lookout for underperforming companies that can be shaken out of their lethargy.

Probably the best known active investor kicking around is Guinness Peat Asset Management but from time to time you will see newspapers refer to others.

Since they are looking for companies that will sit up and take notice, they will inevitably prefer to target smaller companies where building up a decent sized stake is less expensive and is likely to carry more clout.

The sudden appearance of active investors on the company's register will often be accompanied by a rise in the share price, partly because the purchases made to build the stake will have a beneficial effect and partly because shareholders now expect action.

This surge in the share price offers cautious investors the opportunity of getting out while the going is good. It may mean taking an unexpected profit or at least cutting losses after a disappointing slide in the shares over past months.

How can active investors help?

Private investors willing to take a gamble, though, will welcome the attention of active investors. They do not always get it right – no one does – but if they fail to stir management then the situation is unlikely to be any worse than it was before. If they succeed, then the company should produce better profits in future or, as often happens in these circumstances, be the recipient of a takeover offer.

Another tactic that usually works well is to demand that the company be broken up on the grounds that the group would be worth more run as separate discrete businesses rather than as an amalgam of ill-fitting businesses that fail to achieve their individual potential.

Active investors are generally not in for the long term, though they can show extraordinary patience. If they fail to provoke an immediate reaction they will tend to stick around for as long as there is any chance that their investment will pay off.

Just like the rest of us, they are reluctant to admit that they might have got it wrong! However, they tend to think in terms of weeks rather than months and months rather than years.

Active investors are looking for companies that have unfulfilled potential. There is a clear implication that management is falling short in its performance. The active investors may wish to remove some or all of the directors; alternatively, if the current management is seen to have sufficient acumen the idea may be to offer support and guidance.

Sometimes the very appearance of an active investor can be enough to shake executives out of their slumbers and to produce the required improvements. It can also push directors into a state of panic, which is not in anyone's interests.

The worst case scenario is a stand-off where the directors resist the attentions of the active investors and are distracted further from the day-to-day running of the company instead of seeking to correct their faults.

Any investor with 10% or more of the shares has a right to demand an extraordinary general meeting at which the removal of directors can be proposed, which is why an active investor will often build up its stake to around this level. If it comes down to a fight, then there may be a series of expensive, time-consuming EGMs with nothing achieved.

More likely is that the existing management will eventually capitulate, especially if the active investor can gather like-minded supporters or persuade a sizable minority of fellow shareholders to support its cause.

Case study: Photo-Me International

Photography has moved on some way since we first put pound coins into the slot and sat with an inane expression in a railway station booth posing for passport photographs that would prove a source of personal embarrassment for the next 10 years.

The booths are still around, indeed they seem to have proliferated in shopping malls, but they have arguably had their day. The advent of digital cameras has made do-it-yourself photography more appealing and many small pharmacies have taken the opportunity of offering a cheap passport photograph service where the quality of the picture is less open to chance.

On the other hand, making the equipment to process digital photographs has been a growth industry, in sharp contrast to the rapid decline in processing traditional film.

Photo-Me has two strings to its bow. It was in the forefront of making, installing and running photo booths and it subsequently was a leader in making photo laboratories, the equipment for processing digital pictures. This looked to be a promising combination, allowing two bites of the photographic cherry with one side likely to succeed if the other declined or failed to take off.

Alas, Photo-Me seems to have staggered from one setback to another as one side or the other ran into difficulties. The sun last shone in June 2006 when a rise in the share price prompted chairman Vernon Sankey to disclose that Photo-Me had been conducting a strategic review that might lead to an offer being made for the company.

The review rumbled on for months and shareholders were fobbed off with woolly phrases such as, "pursuing strategic options for the individual businesses" and "optimising the capital structure". Takeover talks came to nothing despite "several indications of interest" while the promise of significant return of capital to shareholders was watered down to a proposal to buy back 5% of the shares.

Belatedly, Photo-Me decided it was time to recruit a couple of non-executive directors onto a board that was weighted towards current and former executives.

Two active investors, Principle Capital Fund Managers and QVT Financial, had been building up stakes to a combined 10% and behind the scenes they were campaigning for changes. A lengthy cat and mouse game followed with AGMs being requisitioned then called off and recriminations being issued all round as profits slumped and the proposed sale of the vending division fell through.

Chairman Sankey and Chief Executive Serge Crasnianski were finally forced out.

Chart 12.6: Photo-Me

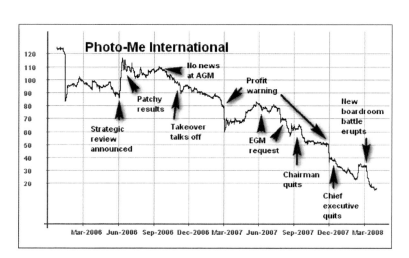

During this period Photo-Me shares slid from 130p at the end of 2005 to a low of just 23p in February 2008.

However, the agony was not yet over. Photo-Me issued two profit warnings in March 2008, pushing the shares down to 15p and prompting Crasnianski, who had retained almost 20% of the shares, and two other former directors with a further 29% to force the resignation of the replacement chairman and two other non-executive directors.

Key points

- The more entrenched the two sides become, the longer the damaging warfare is likely to continue.

- Where trading continues to deteriorate, it is usually best to bite the bullet and sell. That will probably mean taking a loss but hanging on in hope is likely to mean a bigger loss later.

- Read company statements carefully. Does management have a clear idea of what it is doing? Are the strategy statements clear and easy to follow? If you do not understand what the directors are saying, neither will other shareholders – and probably neither do the directors.

- The greater the stake held by the rebels, the more likely they are to prevail. Anything under 10% is a waste of time. Above 10% and an EGM can be demanded – companies are obliged to accede to the request if it is made by shareholders owning at least 10% in total.

- Above 25% blocks any resolution that requires a 75% vote in favour. For instance, many agreed takeovers and mergers are made through what is known as a scheme of arrangement – it is cheaper than a straightforward takeover but needs a 75% vote in favour rather than just 50%.

- When an active shareholder makes demands then backs down, even if only temporarily, management will be encouraged to dig in. At the very least, precious time is lost.

13.

10-Point Checklist

Before we move on to studying individual cases, let us summarise the basics of investing in smaller companies, starting from finding potential candidates to taking the plunge with an investment.

1. Look for possible investments

Read the financial pages in newspapers and websites to find promising small companies. Do your research first rather than rush into investments you may regret. If you miss an opportunity in the meantime, don't worry. There are plenty more out there.

2. Use the internet to check the company's website and other news sources

Look at each company's own website to gather information on what the company does and use search engines to find what has been written about it.

3. Check the sector

Consider whether the company is in a line of business that offers good prospects. Is there heavy competition in the sector or does the company have a unique product? Has it found a niche in the market or does it compete head on with larger rivals? Assess how well the company has performed compared with its competitors.

4. Find which index the company is in

Compare the company's performance against companies of a similar size.

5. Study recent income statements and trading updates

Gain an insight into the past and current performance of the company. Are sales rising? Does the company make a profit? Does it pay a dividend?

6. Study the balance sheet

Confirm that the company is in good financial health. Does it have sufficient cash resources to keep going?

7. Decide how much risk you want to take

Smaller companies tend to offer greater rewards but incur greater risks than larger enterprises. Never risk money that you cannot afford to lose. Decide how long you are prepared to sit on an investment to give it the opportunity to come good.

8. Check liquidity

Use the London Stock Exchange website and financial news websites to determine the normal size of share trades in the company and how frequently shares change hands. Which stock exchange trading platform are share transactions made on? Assess how easy or difficult it will be to buy and sell shares in the company.

9. Build a balanced portfolio

Invest in a range of companies in different sectors. That way you spread the risk while increasing your chances of hitting in a big winner. A portfolio of about 10-12 stocks is manageable for the average investor.

10. Keep your eye on the ball!

Circumstances change … for the whole national economy, for stock market sectors, for individual companies. You don't have to be chopping and changing your portfolio every five minutes but stay alert to what is going on in the marketplace and be prepared to change tack according to how the wind is blowing. If you make a poor investment, be prepared to bite the bullet and cut your losses. If you make a good investment, run with it while the good times roll.

Tax

One final point that may affect your investment decisions is your tax position.

CGT

Capital gains tax is levied on profits from selling shares on the main LSE board; shares in AIM companies are treated as unquoted and capital gains tax is reduced.

IHT

Most AIM stocks are exempt from inheritance tax. The exceptions are those whose business is in land and property; financial activities including banking and insurance; legal services and accountancy; farming and forestry; or managing hotels and nursing homes. While these exceptions seem at first sight to cover a lot of sectors, they still leave plenty to invest in. Banking, insurance and property companies in particular tend to be large companies with a full listing.

This is, admittedly, a benefit for your heirs rather than for you but it is worth remembering in these days when avoiding inheritance tax has become a national sport and all the other obvious loopholes have been closed by Chancellors of the Exchequer in successive Budgets.

ISAs and PEPs

However, the chancellor gets his revenge by refusing to let you put AIM stocks into ISAs or PEPs.

This can be particularly inconvenient if you have in your ISA a main board company that decides to move down to AIM. When a company announces its intention to move down to AIM you are likely to see heavy selling, not only from ISA holders but also from investment and unit trusts that specifically invest only in full listings.

PART III.
Case Studies

14.

Upwardly Mobile

These are the companies we most want to invest in – there are rich pickings to be had from ambitious companies that expand at a steady pace under strong, continuous management.

Don't worry about getting in right at the start of the story. Companies are coming to the market in a constant stream and it is an outright gamble picking the odd one out of hundreds that will ultimately make it all the way to the FTSE 100.

New companies, even the ones that ultimately succeed, will take time to gather momentum so you won't miss out on much if you fail to invest in the early stages. If you do want to back a hunch with a tiny start-up, be prepared to wait for years before your investment really comes good. Rapid gains in share prices come after the company is well established and larger investors start to take notice.

These companies will tend to pay small dividends or make no payout at all in the early stages as they conserve cash to invest in the business. They are therefore initially unattractive to investors seeking an income.

A better option is to look for companies that have already started to gather some momentum. They will have these characteristics:

- They live within their means. Bank borrowings are not stretched too far to fund expansion.

- They establish themselves in one geographic area and expand outwards in an orderly fashion.

- They bring in experienced management as they grow so that existing executives are not overstretched.

- They will often be found in highly fragmented sectors where there are many small players but no big dominating force.

- They usually expand through a mixture of internal growth and buying smaller, privately-owned rivals.

- They are prepared to walk away rather than overpay for an acquisition so these acquisitions tend to be intermittent rather than a regular flow.

- They gain a habit of telling the market that profits will beat expectations.

- They never issue a profit warning out of the blue because the City can be very unforgiving.

Case study: Domino's Pizza

An outstanding success story on AIM has been Domino's Pizza, which operates takeaway and home delivery pizza outlets in the UK and the Republic of Ireland. Although its shares have remained on the junior market, Domino's has grown from a tiny player in a crowded market to being one of the top 50 UK companies quoted on AIM.

Stunning success has come in a comparatively short period of time. The first UK store opened in 1985 in Bedford with the aim of reaching a total of three. There are now over 450 Domino's Pizza stores in a growing number of towns and cities throughout England, Scotland, Wales and Ireland and the current aim is to open 50 new outlets every year.

More than 10,000 staff are employed in the UK and Irish stores in a range of support functions including marketing, IT, training and the production of fresh dough in Milton Keynes and Penrith in England and Naas in Ireland.

The majority of the stores are owned by franchisees who are responsible for delivering the brand's high standards to customers, although some are owned by Domino's itself.

Operating a franchise, where each store is owned by its own manager rather than by the company, is great when it works but the concept is full of dangers. The idea is that the company can grow more quickly, and more cheaply, if it does not have to buy premises and equipment, in this case ovens and delivery vehicles, itself.

Individuals with a bit of entrepreneurial spirit set up their own business within a business, paying a fee for the right to own an exclusive franchise for their own town. These individuals, known as franchisees, incur the start-up costs. In return they are given training and are expected to operate within strict quality controls. The idea is that each outlet will be pretty much like all the others, so customers know what they are getting.

The possible downside with franchising is that training may be inadequate and that franchisees try to go their own way rather than follow the set path of the franchise. It is much harder to get rid of an errant franchisee who is his own boss than to dismiss a recalcitrant employee.

Also the company must take responsibility for marketing and provide full support for its franchisees. While the franchise system tends to attract people with get up and go, not everyone who signs up makes the grade and those who fall short will also get into financial difficulties.

Domino's Pizza clearly got the mix right. Basing its head office in Milton Keynes meant it could spread out in all directions without losing track of its expansion. It has maintained quality control, insisting that pizzas are baked with fresh ingredients and delivered to the customer's door within 30 minutes of the order being placed.

Turnover and profits climbed steadily: turnover doubled from £53m in 2002 to £120m in 2007 while pre-tax profits soared from £4.4m to £18m in the same time frame. Meanwhile, annual dividends have increased from 0.62p to 4.1p.

Chart 14.1: Domino's Pizza

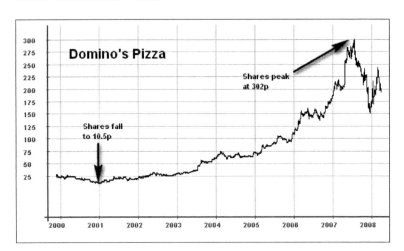

Domino's Pizza shares were just 25p in early 2003. They have been as high as 300p.

Lessons to be learnt

- Smaller companies generally do best when they stick to what they are good at. Domino's had a clear idea that it would operate purely as a takeaway and not try to run restaurants as well, as that would involve an additional set of skills.

- Where a company is supplying fresh ingredients it is particularly important not to overstretch the supply chain. It is best to start from a central point and spread outwards in all directions, never pressing into a new geographical area until existing sites are running satisfactorily.

- Companies that run on a franchise system present extra problems. They must train their franchisees and provide them with full support. If the system works, though, rapid expansion can be achieved without putting a strain on the company's finances.

Case study: Wolseley

Heating and plumbing products supplier Wolseley is another case of a once tiny company growing slowly at first but building the momentum to a higher status. Ultimately, valued at over £3bn, Wolseley in fact made it all the way to the FTSE 100. Yet it began life as a one-man company making sheep shearing machines in Australia in the 19th century and it made its name as a British car manufacturer before yet another transformation saw it become a small engineer and components distributor based in the West Midlands.

Now it is best known in the UK for its Plumb Center outlets but it has built on this chain with a host of similarly named specialist outlets such as Parts Center, Pipe Center and Drain Center. Despite the American spelling, this was originally very much a British company, and a very successful one at that.

At first it followed the trusted path of acquiring smaller similar outfits in a fragmented market. It grew at a sensible pace, building up its coverage of the UK until around the millennium.

However, as Wolseley grew bigger, so did its ambitions. It began to buy businesses in the US and in Europe. Branching into other countries has quite different characteristics from expanding within one's home territory and Wolseley was dragged down by the collapse of the US housing market that sparked the credit crunch.

Shareholders did best while Wolseley was a comparatively small company growing through a mixture of opening new depots and buying small rivals. The problems arrived when Wolseley overstretched itself with international chains that grew out of control and heavy bank borrowings that had to be serviced through the downturn in its markets.

Chart 14.2: Wolseley

Those investors who backed Wolseley in its earlier growth years and beyond have had a rollercoaster ride along with the ups and downs of the building industry that the company serves. For example, in 1998 and 1990 the shares dropped from 550p to below 300p and bounced all the way back up in just over 12 months.

A difficult trading period in early 2000 saw them back below 300p, but ambitious expansion saw them take off again and they ultimately peaked at 1450p in 2006 before the problems in the US took their toll.

Key points

- It is always tempting to stick with a successful company but be alert to the possibility that it may over extend itself. There is no magic formula for knowing when a success story has run its course but as a general rule it is best to get out when surging shares start to fall back equally sharply.

- Warning signs are a high price/earnings ratio and a low yield. That means the shares are pricing in continued growth, possibly at the same pace as in the past, which may be unsustainable.

15.

Niche Players

Speedy Hire, Domino's Pizza and Wolseley thrived as small companies because they found a niche. They established themselves serving specific markets where they could be large fish in small ponds. They also had ambition.

When a company floats on the stock exchange the primary purpose of doing so is to raise money. This may be to allow the founders of the company to cash in on their creation or to raise money for the business itself or a combination of the two.

In the former case, if all the founders want to do is cash in, then one has to ask where the company is going to go from here. The people running the business have got their reward, so how much interest do they have in taking the business further? In the latter case, what is the company going to do with the cash if it is not for expansion?

So it is always worth asking before you invest in a small company: is it going anywhere? If not, what do you hope to gain from such an investment?

Small, unambitious companies may have found a niche for themselves. They may be paying a solid dividend. But the shares are unlikely to make worthwhile gains and if you want to just jog along it may be better to pick a boring large company rather than a boring small company.

Take a good look at the management of a small-and-proud-of-it company. Are the people at the top suitable to be running a quoted company or would they really be happier in charge of a private company that knows its place?

Is the achievement of a stock market quotation the limit of management's ambitions?

Spotting an opportunity

On the other hand, small can be beautiful where a company finds itself a genuine niche in the market.

This can happen where a company comes up with a new product or a new version of an existing product. Getting in first gives the company a head start and if the market for that product is fairly restricted it may not be worthwhile for anyone else to try to muscle in.

Small companies can also find a niche supplying highly specialised products to large international players who do not want to make a commitment to comparatively small scale manufacturing processes.

The motor industry is a prime example of how large international manufacturers are happy to rely on a few hand-picked specialist suppliers of precision components.

For example, TT Industries is a very successful niche manufacturer. It has specialised in making the sensors that have proliferated in modern vehicles. They warn you when you forget to put on your seat belt or set off with the parking brake on. They switch the brakes on and off when a wheel spins and the lights on when it gets dark.

These and many more are vital components that motor manufacturers farm out to suppliers. As the components have become increasingly sophisticated, so it has become sensible to leave their manufacture to specialists producing a limited range rather than for every car maker to commit themselves, their staff and their production lines to every fiddly job.

The oil industry, although even more dominated by giants, has also learnt the value of letting niche players carry out specialist work. For example, rig making is seen as a quite separate industry from actual exploration.

Smaller explorers have also found a niche in exploring out of the way areas or where reserves are thought to be too small to interest the large international integrated oil companies.

There are many industries where niches can be carved out by enterprising small companies. Where this involves supplying goods or services to much larger companies it can be a double edged weapon.

The advantages are a ready market and competing as equals with other small suppliers. The downside is that the small players may be at the mercy of much bigger enterprises that can cut back at short notice. In tough economic times, the big players will attempt to push down the prices of the smaller ones.

Case study: Hornby

Model railways and racing cars specialist Hornby is an excellent example of how a small but ambitious company can cope with difficult trading conditions and actually thrive by adapting to changed circumstances.

Hornby was one of several famous British toy brands such as Meccano and Dinky that were practically wiped out by the flood of cheap competition from the Far East after the Second World War.

One might have expected the arrival of computer and interactive games to apply the coup de grace but Hornby trains, in tandem with Scalextric slot racing systems, have not only made a comeback but they are now having an impact in international markets.

Back in October 2000, as the long bear market at the start of the Millennium was taking hold, you could buy Hornby shares for just 25p. By the time the stock market as a whole hit the bottom in March 2003, Hornby shares had already topped 100p and they powered on to a peak of 305p in January 2007.

There are various reasons for this success but basically they boil down to Hornby taking its opportunities when they arose. The company detected a movement back towards more traditional toys that provided an impetus for a recovery in sales.

Management realised that selling prices had to be held down, though, so manufacturing was moved to low cost centres, particularly China. However, quality control was a key factor, as Hornby could not sell on cheapness alone.

Hornby also embraced the technological age by introducing digitally controlled tracks and rolling stock. It also spotted marketing opportunities, for example by introducing a Hogwarts Express set at the height of Harry Potter's popularity and by signing deals with top Formula 1 racing drivers such as Lewis Hamilton for Scalextric.

Finding markets

The company realised the dangers of being totally dependent on the fickle UK toy market even though it was able to sell to nostalgic dads as well as their children. Australia proved a particularly fertile market but Hornby also took the opportunity of moving into Europe through astute acquisitions, buying brand names that were well known but were living on faded glory, as Hornby itself once had.

Electrotren in Spain and Lima in Italy were bought in 2004, Hornby's distributor in France was acquired the following year and in November 2006 Hornby bought the Airfix model kit business from administrators.

Trading has admittedly had its ups and downs in the meantime but significant growth was reported in the UK market in the run-up to Christmas 2007, helped by a late surge, and European demand was also strong. Orders and sales for January-March, the final quarter of Hornby's financial year, were at a higher level in the UK than the previous year's particularly good performance.

This success did highlight a potential problem that can face successful smaller companies. Introducing new products to meet demand in Europe placed a strain on Hornby's supply chain and steps had to be taken to strengthen management and manufacturing resources.

Chart 15.1: Hornby

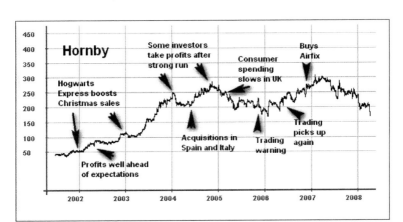

Hornby shares were stuck in the sidings until late 2002 when they finally moved above 50p. They chugged to 278p in November 2004 and after a bout of profit taking finally topped 300p in early 2007.

Key points

- A well known name is not enough but it can certainly help. It is hard to see how the company could have done so well had it not had the Hornby name and it is worth noting that Hornby has taken over ailing companies with similar well known names on the Continent to repeat the winning formula.

- Small companies can source products from low cost manufacturing countries just as many larger ones have done.

- Where the UK market is limited it may be vital to sell abroad as well.

Case study: Manganese Bronze

Having a well known product in a clearly defined niche market with guaranteed demand ought to translate into a thriving small business but this does not always happen.

It is possible for a company to become complacent, to fail to invest in improving its product or be slow to react to encroaching competition.

Manganese Bronze, despite its name implying specialised mining operations, is in fact the company behind the famous London black cabs. Its performance over several years has been bumpy.

Way back in 2002, when Manganese issued monthly figures for the number of taxis sold, data made depressing reading with most months showing a substantial fall in sales. For the 12 months to 31 July 2002 it made a pre-tax loss of nearly £3m for the second year in a row and was forced to slash the dividend from 3p to 1p a share.

Unwelcome distractions

Management had been distracted by two major projects that were costing money as well as time – the company would have been profitable but for the development costs.

One project was Zingo, a system for hailing taxis by using mobile phones. A budget of £8m was allocated. The idea was that Zingo's computer would locate the customer by tracking where the call was coming from and alert the nearest empty taxi using a global positioning system.

Alas, the difficulty of obtaining consistently reliable location data from the mobile phone networks held up the project. It was a delay that Manganese, with limited resources, could ill afford and there was to be a further delay before Zingo was finally launched.

The other major project was the new TXII vehicle with a more efficient diesel engine. An important aspect of this project was a licence agreement for Brilliance China Automotive to make and sell taxis based on the TXII design in China, benefiting from lower local manufacturing costs.

Brilliance made the first royalty payment then changed its management. Payments ceased, so Manganese was drawn into discussions with Brilliance's new bosses to find out what was going on. Eventually the licence deal was terminated.

Meanwhile, Manganese was also busy sorting out problems in its own components division, where loss-making contracts had to be scrapped.

The group finally got back into profit in 2005 after four years of losses and the Zingo cab hailing system finally came good when Computer Cab, a taxi fleet, installed it. Further profit improvements have followed but demand has continued to be volatile.

Chart 15.2: Manganese Bronze

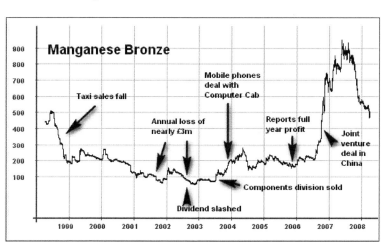

Manganese Bronze's share price held up remarkably well during its trials and tribulations, moving up from a low of 50p in late 2002 to hover around 200p until the middle of 2006.

They then motored to 950p in May 2007 before falling all the way back to around 525p.

Key points

* Manganese Bronze has a very narrow market in the UK and is therefore likely to see demand fluctuate. Given its highly specialised product lines it is hard to gear production up or down to meet these fluctuations.

* Management needs to act quickly when under pressure to take advantage of new opportunities.

* Takeover negotiations can be a serious distraction, especially when a major shareholder is lurking in the background.

Government contracts

Government contracts can provide a healthy source of revenue for smaller companies. All main political parties accept that there is a role for the private sector in providing services for the public sector, including in particular defence, education, health and local authority work.

Pitching for large scale public/private finance projects is costly and time consuming, with no guarantee of success if three or four companies are competing for the contract. However, smaller companies can often subcontract work from the winner of the main contract and they can also pick up smaller contracts in their own right. The key is to provide a good service at reasonable cost.

Public sector bodies are keen to keep prices down but that is not the only criterion – the work has to be up to scratch. Local authorities in particular would rather stick with a proven service provider, especially one with the required specialised knowledge and experience, than risk an unknown cheaper one.

Public sector bodies have big budgets and are highly unlikely to default. They typically seek to sign three or five year deals and may even offer contracts as long as ten years so there is a guaranteed stream of income.

On the other hand, budgets can be tight, especially towards the end of the financial year when projects may be deferred.

Case study: Manpower Software

Manpower Software provides computer programmes for planning work rosters. This is a highly specialised niche that is unlikely to attract the attentions of larger software developers but there is a need for sophisticated products.

Many employers of large numbers of staff need to be able to plan 24 hour services seven days a week, allowing for shift working, days off and holiday entitlements. Sectors using Manpower Software products include its traditional markets of military and maritime plus healthcare, which was added in 2002.

Maintaining correct staffing at a level that is adequate but not unnecessarily high is critical so the software has to be proven and reliable. A well established small company charging reasonable prices can effectively corner this kind of market, making it difficult for a new rival to break in.

Despite being a small company, Manpower Software has been able to sell abroad and its clients include NATO, the military alliance of Western nations.

There was an anxious hiatus in 2006 when the company swung into a loss. It had spent to strengthen key personnel to improve sales and the benefits had not yet come through.

Manpower's management felt that the group had superior products, an impressive customer base and a strong workforce of its own but great care was needed to secure the future. It was important to hold down spending where possible but to invest where profit margins were greater. In particular, one-off software sales had to be followed up with revenue from continuing licences over a number of years to guarantee future income.

Crucially, Manpower had sufficient cash reserves to keep going in the meantime.

A stream of contract wins, many of them small in themselves but adding up in aggregate, augured well for the future and Manpower was back in the black with interim profits for the six months to 30 November 2006. Profitability has since improved further.

Another good sign was that Ian Bowles, who became chief executive in May 2007, bought shares in the company even before he joined it. Chairman Terry Osborne also raised his stake, as did an outside adviser to the company.

Chart 15.3: Manpower Software

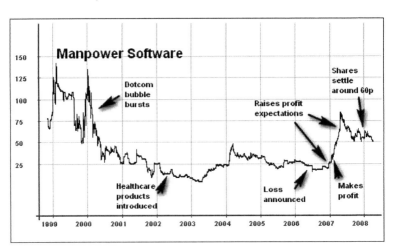

Manpower's shares have risen strongly on two separate occasions since the stock market hit the bottom in early 2003. They had understandably slumped when the dotcom bubble burst and technology projects were abandoned but from a meagre 2.5p they raced up to 48p over a 12 month period.

After three years of drifting they were back below 20p but the successful turning round of the company propelled them to 84p in early 2007. They drifted again over several months before consolidating around 60p.

Key points

- Government policy has swung towards giving smaller companies a chance to win contracts. It was a central message of Alistair Darling's first Budget as Chancellor of the Exchequer in March 2008. While politicians do not always do as they say, there is clearly scope for niche players serving the public sector.

- Supplying specialised products that work well is often a good way to win government contracts.

Going green

Green issues, as everyone knows, are coming into their own. The rise of China and India as consumer nations, exacerbated by China's inefficient manufacturing processes, has put an intolerable strain on the supply of raw materials.

Food prices have also risen, not only because of increased consumption in two nations that together make up a third of global population but also because of the search for biofuels that has taken some land out of food production and into growing alternative fuels.

The notion of green investments has been around for 20 years or more but it has been slow to take off. Companies have in the past paid lip service to the idea and made cosmetic changes but anyone who unwraps their groceries after a visit to the supermarket knows how much packaging is wasted. Goods are still transported excessive distances before they reach the shops.

Greenery is at last opening up opportunities and some small businesses have seen the opportunity to establish green credentials. It is an area where being small and nimble rather than large and lumbering can pay off.

Going green has, however, been full of pitfalls, whatever the potential advantages. It has involved developing new technology which may be beyond the means of smaller businesses, either in terms of cost or technical know-how.

There is also the problem of persuading other companies, often larger ones, to take the greener products. Wind farms, for instance, must sell their output into the National Grid. Makers of biodegradable wrapping need to convince food manufacturers to switch from traditional packaging.

Green alternatives are not necessarily cheaper now, though they may well be in the future if demand, and therefore prices, for traditional products outstrips supply.

In other words, green investments offer considerable scope but they need to be treated with special care. Investors should consider whether an idea is a fad or a vital part of saving the world. They need to consider how long it will take for revenue to start rolling in, let alone profits.

Go with your conscience if you must but green investment can be a rocky ride. Shareholders in start-ups may need to be very patient. On the other hand, there have been opportunities to leap on a bandwagon. Just remember the need to jump off when a bandwagon starts to roll backwards.

Case study: Clipper Windpower

Creating electricity by harnessing the wind is a great idea in theory. There is plenty of wind and there are exposed places to take advantage of it, but the spread of wind farms, on and off shore, has been controversial.

Proponents point to the use of a renewable source of power with free fuel stock. There are no carbon dioxide or other emissions to pollute the atmosphere or break up the ozone layer. The hope is that we can avoid having to build a new series of nuclear power stations with their inherent risk of long term radioactivity.

Critics argue that wind turbines are much more expensive than the makers admit and that their life span is short. They are unreliable in that they work only when there is sufficient wind and therefore conventional or nuclear power stations must be kept running anyway to make up any shortfall.

Whatever the merits of the rival arguments, Clipper Windpower was greeted enthusiastically when it joined AIM in September 2005, raising £75m in a share placing. It was one of the largest AIM flotations that year.

Founded in 2001, Clipper Windpower designs wind turbines and develops and owns wind farms. It has developed its own advanced wind turbine technology and its C-93 Liberty turbine has been installed in its projects and sold to third parties. It had already put together a substantial portfolio of sites for wind farm development by the time its shares joined AIM, with potential capacity totalling over 5,800MW.

Winning contracts

The following July Clipper announced an exciting deal: a five-year project with oil giant BP. Wind farms with a total generating capacity of 2,015MW would be located in New York, Texas, and South Dakota.

As part of the joint venture, BP's alternative energy arm committed to buy up to 900 Liberty turbines for use on other projects in BP's global wind business.

More contracts followed in 2007 as the desire to be seen as green grew along with the price of oil. These included an extension of an existing agreement to supply wind turbines to California-based Edison Mission Group and a new deal with Minnesota Power for the first large scale wind energy project to be built in northern Minnesota.

Despite receiving firm orders for 181 turbines for delivery in 2007 and 311 for 2008, Clipper reported a first half loss in 2007 due to production costs and what it called 'procurement inefficiencies and legacy sales pricing'. In other words, as a small and comparatively new company Clipper had initially lacked the clout to secure supplies and raise its prices.

Unfortunately, later that year Clipper was conducting tests when it found a fault in a part from a supplier that could shorten its working life. A number of previously installed turbines were potentially affected and shipments of new turbines were slowed.

In all, the setback would cost up to £8m over 6-12 months. Some blades also had to be replaced early and compensation was due to customers for late delivery.

Even coming into 2008, Clipper was able to raise prices only modestly and it was forced to seek a cash injection from a private equity investor.

Chart 15.4: Clipper Windpower

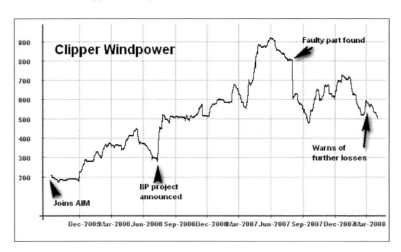

With this mixed bag of news, investors have blown hot and cold over the shares. They shot up from around 200p soon after the float to a peak just over 900p in May 2007 but news of first half losses followed by production problems dragged them all the way back to 477p within four months. A recovery to 700p petered out as Clipper reported that there would be a second half loss similar to the first half pre-tax deficit of $77.8m.

Clipper's costs seemed to have run ahead much faster than its revenue and it needed to ramp up its prices sharply to make a profit, something that was proving difficult to do.

Key points

- Going green is fine – in fact it will be an increasingly important factor in business – but do not invest blindly in companies involved in green issues. You still need to make out an investment case for each one.

- Whatever the merits of saving the planet, other companies may be less enthusiastic. Selling green products does not guarantee that there will be a market for them.

Case study: D1 Oils

The humble jatropha tree holds the key to the future of D1 Oils, a provider of biofuel for road transport that has been slow to live up to initial hopes.

D1 floated in October 2004 with a prospectus outlining plans for low cost biofuel production on 37,000 hectares of plantations in Africa, India and the Philippines. It had options on an additional 6m hectares.

The jatropha is native to India and it can grow on wasteland. Alternative energy enthusiasts claim it can produce over 2,000 barrels of oil per square mile each year.

D1 Oils set out to exploit this potential by creating alliances with associate companies in India that would grow the bushes while D1 marketed the harvest. Early signs were good.

One associate, Aavin Dairies, grew jatropha trees on 300 hectares in Tamil Nadu using fertilizer supplied by D1 and the trees reached the oil bearing stage within a year of planting, more than six months ahead of expectation.

An agreement was signed to form a joint venture in China, 51% owned by D1 Oils, that would not only grow the plants but would have a refinery able to produce 20,000 tonnes of biodiesel a year. The £2.5m start-up costs would be financed entirely by the Chinese. The Indian government granted a licence for the export of jatropha seeds for use in China and elsewhere.

Announcing these initiatives at the end of 2004, chairman Karl Watkin enthused:

These agreements mark a significant step in the evolution of D1 Oils, its brand and supply chain. China and Asia Pacific represent large, exciting markets for biodiesel backed by government initiatives in combating climate change and dependence on foreign fuel.

Just two month later D1 announced it was expanding in Madagascar, having spotted 17,000 hectares of existing jatropha plantations and made arrangements to harvest the output.

The trees were being used as supports for growing vanilla but D1 was well placed to harness their potential.

Chart 15.5: D1 Oils

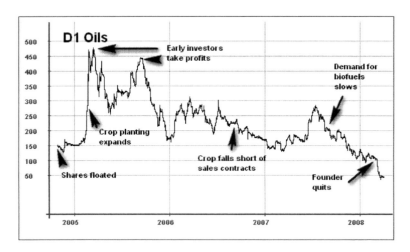

With everything in the garden lovely, D1 shares motored from an initial 150p to a peak of 475p in less than five months but canny investors took their profits, fearing that the shares had run away too quickly given that these were early days.

D1 still had to demonstrate that it could grow, harvest and refine oil in sufficient quantities and find markets.

News flow started to look generally encouraging with more hectares brought into production and refining capacity at Middlesbrough and overseas coming on stream, but the success in selling output had an unfortunate consequence. With supplies from jatropha trees insufficient to meet the amount of refined oil that D1 had contracted to supply, it was necessary to buy in expensive vegetable oil in 2006 to make up the shortfall.

D1's share price graph shows a series of surges on hopes that the company would be taken over followed by a decline to ever lower troughs, with the shares dropping below 100p for the first time in early 2008.

The group had in the meantime run up increasing losses as cash was ploughed into the expanding operations.

It decided to withdraw from its UK refining business, a decision that meant writing down the value of assets by £22.8m, and like Clipper was forced to raise more cash to keep going, in this case through a placing of 64.4m new shares at 25p each, a 34% discount to the then stock market price of 37.75p.

Key points

- It can take time for a green idea to translate into reality and it is vital that there are sufficient cash reserves to keep the company going until revenue starts to flow. Any business based on agriculture has a natural time delay from planting to harvesting that can last months or years depending on the crop.

- A green company may be at the mercy of manufacturers who need to be convinced of the need to adapt their products.

Case study: 888

A classic example of the dangers of being too heavily dependent on one product in one major market was also provided by the online gambling sector.

Internet poker playing is currently illegal in the United States (under the 1932 Wire Act – the 'wire' in question being telephone wires). Not to worry. If online gambling companies could not set up on US soil, then it was perfectly simple to establish headquarters in Antigua or Gibraltar and collect the bets from there.

When the internet arrived, there was no need for a physical presence. The ether brought gamblers together from all over the world – but especially from the US, where more enterprising residents found a way round gambling prohibition just as they had defied alcohol prohibition back in the days when the Wire Act was passed to curb organised crime.

Gambling in any circumstances requires a ready pool of players. You can't bet against yourself and the more successful internet sites were the ones that always had a game on the go for those logging on to join in.

The American gambling industry, fearing a threat to Las Vegas and US race tracks, set out on a protectionist campaign. It was not clear whether the Wire Act applied to internet betting. After all, the law was passed way before the internet was thought of. That did not stop law enforcement officers from states such as Louisiana from issuing arrest warrants for executives of overseas-based internet gambling companies.

After two high profile arrests when unfortunate directors from rival internet betting companies were in transit at American airports, the game was clearly up and a law specifically banning internet gaming by US citizens was signed by President George Bush in October 2006. The law used the simple expedient of banning banks and credit companies from passing cash from American gamblers to the gaming companies.

Recovery plans

Among the companies forced to close their US links was 888, which had previously received more than half its revenue from US players. It had been clear for several months that a ban was likely and, in common with its rivals, 888 had been actively recruiting subscribers elsewhere.

However, the company admitted that suspension of US activities would have "a material adverse impact on results for this year and beyond". In fact, 888 saw $43.3m profits from the US disappear in the first half of 2007.

Measures to reduce fixed costs were rapidly put in place and 888 pointed out that it had built up a cash pile to keep the operations going.

Acting quickly, 888 stuck a deal with Georgica, the owner of Rileys, the UK's largest chain of 168 snooker, pool and poker clubs, to provide online poker on Rileys' website and in its clubs. In separate deals, 888 bought an online bingo business and launched into South America.

New games such as backgammon were introduced and a sports licence was obtained in Italy. However, talks with bookmaker Ladbrokes on a takeover offer for 888 foundered after several months of haggling.

Chart 15.6: 888

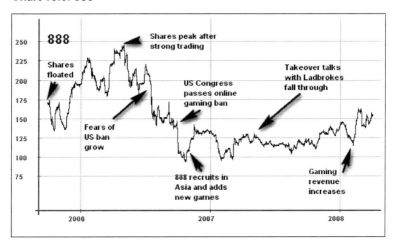

Shares in 888 were floated at 170p in late 2005 and they peaked at 245p the following May. The US ban saw them plunge below 100p. With the group taking measures to expand business elsewhere, including Asia, the shares have since settled around 125p.

Although 888 has lost its most lucrative market, it has secured a much wider base that could ultimately provide better foundations. It was able to report that it had more than doubled full year profits from continuing operations in 2007, its first full year of trading since abandoning its US-facing operations.

Key points

- There were plenty of warnings that the US would clamp down on online gaming months before it actually happened. These signs were ignored by many investors and some of the companies involved in the vain hope that the problem would go away.

- Companies with one major market are at risk if problems arise in that market.

- Tribulations can be turned to advantage if a company is forced into taking remedial action. Look for any company whose share price has been punished but which is coping and could bounce back over time.

16.

Competing With The Big Boys

It is possible for smaller companies to compete head on with larger ones but it is a dangerous game.

The larger ones are likely to have a wider breadth of more experienced management. They can reduce costs by demanding better terms from suppliers and they tend to be taken more seriously by their customers. Large companies usually have more marketing muscle and are more able to put cash into research and development.

Small fish in a big pool therefore need some characteristic that makes them stand out from the crowd.

This may be a specialised product that tackles a part of the market that larger companies may feel is not worth putting resources into. It may be producing higher quality that customers are prepared to pay for. It could involve serving a geographic region where larger companies are poorly represented.

One big advantage that smaller companies can have is an ability to react quickly to demand.

However you look at it, small companies competing against large ones need some attribute that merits your investment.

Case study: Air Partner

Air Partner saw a niche for supplying executive jets as an area where larger commercial operators would be unlikely to compete. While it has been a turbulent ride, with profits bouncing up and down according to the prevailing wind, it has certainly been a successful one overall.

The company has had two main strands to its business. The more reliable and steady one has been providing jets for routine business travel. This service is particularly useful for small and medium sized companies that have business abroad, particularly in Europe and the Middle East, but cannot justify the cost of maintaining their own private jet.

Smaller aircraft can fly into smaller airfields. Air Partner exploited the fact that time-conscious executives could be flown nearer to city centres and to provincial towns, cutting out travel times to and from airports. Long check-in waits were avoided, likewise waiting for baggage at the other end.

Hiring Air Partner jets could be very cost effective and could impress a company's clients.

The second strand produced a less certain flow of business, although it brought Air Partner to the attention of prospective customers and proved its reliability. The jets could be used in emergencies to fly stranded overseas workers out of trouble zones wherever violence flared up.

Again, small aircraft could be sent close to where they were needed and use short grass runways or whatever flat land was available.

This line of business was characterised by long lulls punctuated by bouts of frantic activity. It meant that Air Partner had to have arrangements where it could lay its hands on necessary aircraft and flying crew at short notice. However, companies with oil or minerals exploration in remote, politically unstable regions were willing to pay a regular premium to ensure that help was at hand at the first sign of trouble.

Any investor taking the trouble to look back through results announcements and trading statements issued since Air Partner was formed in 1999 will see how up and down profits have been. The company surely holds the record for the number of times it has had to alert the stock market to the fact that it would either beat or fall short of expectations.

Doing the right things

In all this time two factors worked in Air Partners favour. It was prompt and upfront in issuing this guidance so shareholders could feel confident that they knew where they stood.

Equally important, Air Partner had two top executives who worked well together. Tony Mack was executive chairman and David Savile was managing director. Such an arrangement can be a recipe for friction and it runs counter to what is normally regarded as best practice in a quoted company: having a non-executive chairman to balance a chief executive.

It is essential in an arrangement such as the one at Air Partner that the respective duties are clearly designated, that there is no doubt which is the senior executive and that the two at the top clearly understand and respect each other. This seems to have been the case over several years at Air Partner and it was especially important given the uncertain nature of earnings.

Air Partner has spread internationally but has done so step by step without overstretching itself. It now has 21 offices in 12 countries in Europe, the US, Asia and the Middle East. It signed an 80 year lease for a £5m development at Biggin Hill in Kent, just 14 miles from the City of London, where it manages Western Europe's largest fleet of Lear jets.

From time to time Mack has sold part of his substantial shareholding to institutions. This has had several beneficial effects. Firstly, it reduced his dominance of the share register so the company is less likely to be seen as too much under his control.

Secondly, it increased liquidity in the shares by spreading ownership. This liquidity could not be satisfied by issuing new shares as Air Partner did not need to raise cash for development.

Because the shares were placed rather than sold in the market, it meant that Mack has divested himself without depressing the share price. This was important given that Mack was heading towards retirement in 2008 and might wish to reduce his stake considerably after the group passed into someone else's stewardship.

Finally, the fact that institutional investors were clamouring for shares was a key vote of confidence in the company.

Chart 16.1: Air Partner

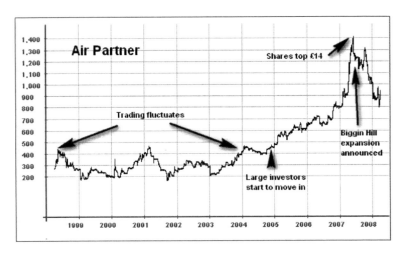

Air Partner shares bounced around between 200p and 500p until the beginning of 2005, reflecting the fluctuating performance over several years. As the company became increasingly noticed by larger investors, the shares gradually gathered upward momentum and eventually peaked at 1400p just after the Biggin Hill expansion was announced.

Global economic concerns then started to take their toll and the shares settled back to find a floor just below 900p in early 2008. The announcement that Mack was to retire as soon as a replacement could be found may also have prompted some profit taking.

Savile stepped up to chief executive, which means the company will still be run by someone who knows it backwards, and a non-executive chairman was appointed in April 2008, bringing Air Partner into line with what is regarded as best practice.

At the same time Air Partner announced a 12% rise in interim profits for the six months to January 2008 and said current trading was meeting full-year expectations, although its private jet operation had experienced evidence of 'corporate belt-tightening'.

Key points

- Two heads can be better than one – provided the top two get on together.

- Continuity at the top is important in a specialist business.

- When trade fluctuates sharply from year to year it is easier to survive the difficult times if the company is not overstretched.

Case study: Silverjet

While links between giant national flag carriers have characterised the airline industry in recent years, Silverjet attempted to carve out a niche for itself as an executive airline flying on a very small scale.

So small, in fact, that it began life with just one aircraft flying just one route, Luton to New York. The big attraction was that all the seats converted into beds. Still, former airline start-ups such as easyJet and Ryanair had grown to become industry giants and their backers had made a lot of money on the way.

Silverjet had the potential of filling the gap left by the scrapping of Concorde: if executives could no longer make short supersonic transatlantic crossings then they could have the compensation of comfort in place of speed.

The major issue was whether such a business plan could be viable. Silverjet had to invest £50m in start-up costs, creating 300 jobs. Aircraft are expensive and fuel costs have risen. Converting the planes to hold fewer passengers, each with more space, meant that planes had to fill a higher percentage of available seats to break even.

Initially having just one plane allowed little room for manoeuvre. On one occasion a mechanical problem forced Silverjet to find alternative carriers to bring its passengers home. Such an event not only attracted adverse publicity: it also negated the concept of a stress-free flight.

Nonetheless, Silverjet added a second schedule, between London and Dubai. Given the emergence of the Middle Eastern territory as a major economic centre as well as an oil kingdom, there was excellent scope for attracting the type of passenger that forms Silverjet's clientele.

By early 2008, Silverjet had a fleet of three 100-seat Boeing 767s flying twice a day to New York and daily to Dubai with two more aircraft on order. It managed to fill 54% of its seats in January and strong bookings for the following month and beyond suggested that passenger numbers would continue to rise.

No leeway

However, just as the omens were more encouraging, Silverjet shares were hit by a particularly critical piece of analysis issued by stockbroker Daniel Stewart. It was not just that Stewart advised its clients to sell: the broker argued that Silverjet shares were worthless as "the business model doesn't work and we can't see that it ever will".

Although Silverjet had revenue, Stewart analyst Mike Stoddart feared that it would eventually run out of cash.

Meanwhile British Airways, with more places, more cash and more marketing muscle, unveiled plans to launch a rival service with only business between London and New York.

Small companies with a great idea, such as Silverjet's, will always be at the mercy of larger outfits that wait to see if a service or product works before wading in with an alternative.

Silverjet was caught in a dilemma over pricing. Its return fares of £1,099 were too high to attract ordinary travellers but were not high enough to produce sufficient income to make the airline viable.

Chart 16.2: Silverjet

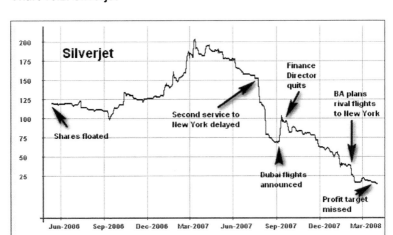

Silverjet shares peaked at 200p in March 2007 but slid all the way to 12.5p in March 2008. Takeover hopes then pushed them briefly to 21p before attempts to raise cash to keep going failed and Silverjet was forced to cease flying, lay off staff and suspend trading in its shares.

Key points

• Taking on the big boys is all very well if you have a product that differentiates you but any small company is vulnerable to larger rivals muscling in on its patch.

• Large companies may let small companies take the risks and incur the start-up costs of setting up a new service or product. Once the new line is proved to work, larger rivals can move in to snatch the rewards. Often the best that the smaller company's investors can hope for is to see their company taken over. This can prove cheaper for the larger rival than setting up a competing business.

Exploration companies

Small exploration companies represent a particular challenge and are generally to be regarded as particularly high risk but potentially high reward investments.

Mining is a particularly tricky area, whatever the size of the company. The merits of a particular mine or smelter will vary according to the price of the resource being extracted and how heavily the mineral is concentrated in the ore. Quite small concentrations can be commercially viable if the selling price is right but even experts can get the maths wrong.

Investors should be ultra careful in doing their research, not only into the company they propose to buy shares in but also into the metal itself. Mining companies make announcements that are barely comprehensible outside the industry: beware of investing in anything you don't understand.

Metals, precious stones and oil can turn up in areas of considerable political instability. Even where a country is not involved in civil war or a rebellion – and expensive resources are often seen as worth fighting over – exploration and mining companies can be the targets of insurgents, as even oil giant Shell has discovered in Nigeria.

Exploration tends to involve considerable expense and possibly delays before production and, finally, revenue starts to come in. Promising prospects can end in disappointment when initial indications of underground reserves prove to be less extensive than hoped. Where sufficient reserves are found, geological problems may make production uneconomic.

Agreements with national governments must be negotiated and it will usually be necessary to allow some form of local participation in the project. This is likely to mean that the foreign explorer provides the capital and the expertise, while subsequently having to share the rewards.

Large companies have more negotiating power and more financial backing to survive until output begins. They are in a better position to walk away from a project and concentrate their energies elsewhere.

Price fluctuations

Another factor is the fluctuating price of commodities. Just as office developers are tempted to buy expensive land when commercial property rents are high, only to find that there is a glut of space by the time the building is up and ready for occupancy, so are exploration companies tempted to develop mines and wells in obscure places at times of high commodity prices only to start production just as selling prices start to fall.

The highs and lows of oil and gold prices are well documented but base metal prices have been just as volatile. For example, world demand for copper has soared with the emergence of China and India, which together account for one-third of the world population, as developing industrial nations with growing consumer demand.

This does still leave scope for smaller explorers to capitalise on smaller projects in more out of the way places, always bearing in mind the risks involved. Look to see if a resources company indicates the cost per ounce or per barrel of getting the stuff out of the ground and transporting it to the nearest port or pipeline. This will give an indication of the viability of the project if commodity prices fall and of its potential profitability if prices rise.

Oil exploration does offer a particular opportunity for smaller companies. Large operations such as BP and Shell will often abandon a well as production starts to dry up but before all the oil is extracted. Their large scale operations make small scale output uneconomic.

Smaller companies can and do take over dying wells, buying them cheaply from larger explorers. In fact, the oil industry is much more geared to production sharing than with other commodities and it is quite common for ownership of oil fields to be shared and for stakes to be traded between explorers. This can reduce the risk that smaller companies have to take.

Case study: Cluff Gold

Cluff Gold started gold production at the Angovia mine in Cote d'Ivoire in early February 2008 and was at that time close to starting production at the Kalsaka mine in Burkina Faso. Further exploration was continuing around both these mines and also at Cluff's key Baomahun project in Sierra Leone.

This was pretty good timing given that the price of gold had soared above $900 and then $1,000 as investors sought a safe haven during the worst of the credit crunch.

The two mines coming into production had the potential to transform Cluff's fortunes with 50,000 oz of gold expected to be mined in 2008. In themselves they looked likely to have a comparatively short life so their importance was to provide Cluff with a steady stream of earnings while further exploration was carried out around them and also at Baomahun.

Thus Cluff would be less likely to need to raise fresh capital, either by imposing a rights issue on its shareholders or by diluting existing holdings through bringing in new investors. After raising £6.5m when the shares were floated on AIM in a placing at the end of 2004, Cluff made two further share placings, in December 2005 and in March 2006.

On the other hand, most if not all the income would be swallowed up in further exploration so it would not make cash available yet for the payment of a dividend.

Cluff had a number of other projects at an earlier stage of development. These could provide a stream of encouraging news announcements if all went well, though there was always the risk of some disappointment.

Chart 16.3: Cluff Gold

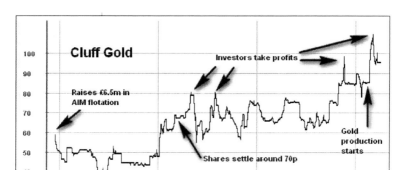

Cluff Gold shares have followed an unusual pattern since the company was floated in a placing at 55p in late 2004. They slipped from an initial 60p to trade around 50p for virtually the whole of 2005. Then they settled erratically around 70p for nearly two years before briefly topping 100p towards the end of 2007 and settling around a new level at 90p.

It does look as if some shareholders have taken the opportunity to pocket some profits after each surge, possibly buying back in on the dips. Certainly the shares have provided plenty of scope for active investors to bob in and out.

This has been an investment for those who combine patience with speculation. Losses have increased, though not dramatically, from £1.1m in the 2004 calendar year to £1.4m in 2005 and £1.9m in 2006.

Key points

- Shares in exploration companies can be quite volatile and offer opportunities for short-term traders cashing in on sharp share price movements as well as for long-term investors willing to ride out the peaks and the troughs.

- Exploration companies are vulnerable to fluctuations in commodity prices that can make a particular exploration suddenly viable or uneconomic. That is in addition to the possibility that a mine or oil well may contain more or less than initial drilling results suggest.

- Mining companies with sufficient cash to fund exploration and development are at an advantage although it may still take some time before a dividend is paid.

Case study: Braemore Resources

The ups and downs of being a niche player in the mining sector, where companies are dependent on fluctuating metal prices as well as their relationship with larger companies, is amply demonstrated at Braemore Resources.

The shares began life at a mere 2.5p in March 2005 and rapidly advanced to 15p, nice work for those who got in at the start. They drifted downwards then sideways for the next couple of years before surging briefly to 14p in June 2007. This time the doldrums lasted just four months before rising metal prices pushed the stock from 10p in mid-October to 23p a month later.

Braemore came into existence in 2005 when it bought out an Australian company, Western Consolidated Nickel. The principal activities of the group were to evaluate the reclamation and processing of sulphide nickel tailings at BHP Billiton's nickel operations at Leinster, Mt Keith and Kambalda in Western Australia.

Given its limited financial resources, Braemore issued up to 600m of its shares in payment for the acquisition and set about raising £3m to finance the necessary work.

The lure was the claim that, at prevailing London metal prices, there could be as much as £3bn worth of nickel in the ground and Braemore actually raised £4.2m in a placing within a month, mainly through London-based financial institutions.

There was a ready buyer for the nickel, as BHP Billiton signed an exclusive agreement to purchase all nickel produced.

Test drilling took longer than expected but results were encouraging and spending on a test plant was less costly than Braemore had allowed for.

Coping with losses

With no income other than interest on cash at the bank, Braemore continued to run at a loss until June 2006.

In December 2006 Braemore took a strategic decision to take control of Independence Platinum, an unlisted company registered in England and Wales but with smelting operations in South Africa.

This took made the company less dependent on Australia and less dependent on nickel. Although Independence did refine nickel, it also produced copper and the expensive metals in the platinum range.

The acquisition was financed through the £7.7m placing of shares at 6p in January 2007. The placing, again in London, meant that Braemore probably had adequate resources to see it through to profitability. It also meant that Atomaer Holdings, the Australian company that sold Western Consolidated Nickel to Braemore, no longer held a majority stake.

There was still some way to go though. At the end of March 2008 the group announced a loss of just over £1m in the six months to the end of December 2007, nearly double the loss in the corresponding six months of 2006. Administrative expenses had ballooned from £362,000 to £1.2m.

Chart 16.4: Braemore

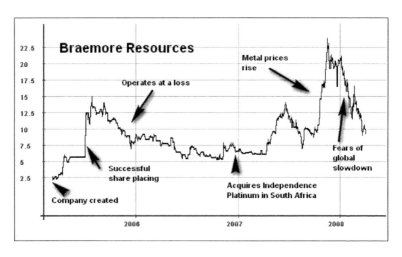

Braemore shares looked to be taking off in the second half of 2007 as they tripled from 7p to 23p but the downturn was also severe and the shares were back to penny stock status by March 2008.

Key points

- Share prices for fledgling mining companies can be very volatile, especially for penny stocks.

- Buying out part of an existing large company is particularly risky. Why does the large company want to sell? Are the assets ever going to make money? Why would a smaller company do better with them?

- It helps if there is a ready buyer for the output already in existence but watertight agreements need to be in place.

- A small specialised company may be a safer investment if it can diversify its risks.

Case study: Hardy Oil

Exploration group Hardy Oil & Gas has certainly been upwardly mobile in a sector where a fair amount of luck is required.

Since it joined AIM at 144p in June 2005 it was blessed with rising prices for its products and a successful exploration programme. By the time it moved up to a full listing in February 2008 the shares had reached 600p, four times their initial value.

The promotion to the main board was warmly greeted, with Hardy shooting to a new high at 635p on a day when shares generally fell. That put the shares on an amazing rating of 280 times prospective earnings – not bad for a company that had yet to pay a dividend!

However, Hardy was still a small company in terms of market capitalisation. With 62.3m shares in issue, it was valued at just £372m.

Even at that stage Hardy was producing oil from only one well, the PY-3 oilfield offshore at Tamil Nadu in India. Oil was flowing at 3,200 barrels a day. As the exploration was shared, a common practice in oil exploration to spread costs and risks, Hardy's share was 580 barrels a day but it was looking to double that by the end of 2009.

Hardy also had assets in Nigeria and it had discovered gas off the east coast of India.

The rationale for joining the main stock market board was that Hardy wanted to raise more cash to fund drilling, both for appraisal and, where there were oil shows, for moving into production. In May 2007 Hardy placed nearly 5m shares at 423p each, raising £21m, but clearly much more was needed.

Chart 16.5: Hardy Oil

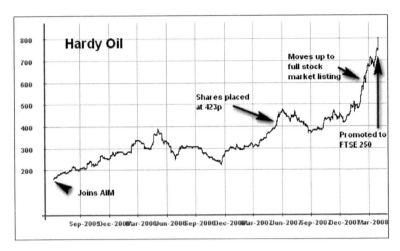

That proved no deterrent to investors and as the shares reached 700p at the start of March 2008 Hardy was included in the FTSE 250 index of midcap stocks in the quarterly review that determines membership of the various indices.

Pre-tax profits for the 2007 calendar year, released in April 2008, showed pre-tax profits down from $13.4m in 2006 to $10.6m thanks to a sharp reduction in production and an increase in the Indian government's share of the proceeds.

This disappointment was offset somewhat by a gain of $10.2m from the sale of shares in Hindustan Oil Exploration.

Key points

- Exploration companies often need to raise more money in order to get their assets into production. Shareholders face a choice between stumping up more cash or seeing their holdings diluted if they decline to take up their rights.

- Investors need to check how much cash an early stage exploration company has and how quickly that cash is being burnt up. Such companies often make clear when they come to market if they are likely to need to raise more funds in due course.

- It is important for explorers to have several projects on the go so that they are not over dependent on just one asset. This need to spread risks is admittedly less urgent if the main project is actually in product as at least there is some income. Mines and wells run out sooner or later, though, so new projects need to be coming on stream to keep income flowing in the future.

Case study: Pan Andean Resources

Oil explorer Pan Andean has been one of life's recurring disappointments. Although it has managed to produce a small pre-tax profit for several years it has failed to take off and revenue has fallen back.

Pan Andean, as its name implies, was set up to find oil and gas in remote (or frontier, as it preferred to call them) areas of South America. It gained notoriety in the 1990s for raising money to drill in what seemed to be a highly promising field that had to be abandoned when the promised oil failed to materialise.

The company claimed that the oil really had been there all the time but it had run away underground across a national barrier in between the cash raising and the drilling and was now sitting out of reach in a neighbouring country.

Pan Andean's reputation never fully recovered from the ribald response in the press to this misfortune. Some unkind journalists suggested the oil had never been there in the first place.

Slow progress

Whatever the truth of the matter, Pan Andean virtually came to a standstill as oil prices fell, making the concessions it owned in Bolivia uneconomic. The group ticked by on a shoestring, with executives checking alternative prospects in countries adjacent to Bolivia and in Africa and the Middle East.

Assurances were still forthcoming as shareholders waited in hope rather than expectation. Oil and gas had been discovered (alas, by other producers) directly to the south and east of Pan Andean's Chapare oil exploration block in Central Bolivia.

The long awaited gas pipeline from Santa Cruz in Bolivia to Sao Paolo in Brazil prompted a claim that demand for gas was so strong in Brazil that the world economic downturn at the end of the millennium would not seriously affect growth in the country.

Despite the hyperbole, prices for any gas that Pan Andean could have produced were too low and no revenue was earned in the year to March 2000 as the company preferred to sit and wait for better times.

It did look as if the corner had been turned when revenue almost reached £5m in the following 12 months but that has not been repeated and pre-tax profits only once topped £1m in a financial year despite steadily rising oil and gas prices.

Exploration results have been patchy, though that is not necessarily a criticism of Pan Andean, more a reflection of the tough life in the world of oil and gas exploration.

Interests have been acquired in the Gulf of Mexico, Texas, Colombia and Peru and the possibility of producing in Iran, the world's fourth biggest oil nation, has been considered.

Chart 16.6: Pan Andean

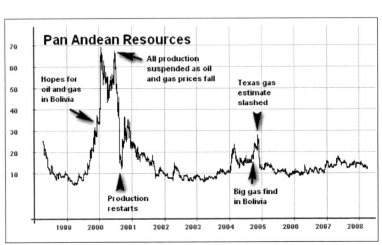

Pan Andean shares have reflected the lack of progress. Apart from two surges to 68p in 2000 in a triumph of hope over adversity, they have spent most of their time below 20p and have on three separate occasions over the years languished in single figures.

Key points

- The stock market can be very slow to forgive. Once a company has disappointed the City it will be a long time before it is taken seriously again, even if management changes.

- Exploration results can be patchy even when companies seem to be looking in the right places. There is no substitute for getting production on stream.

Tech stocks

Smaller companies can compete in the high-tech world, even if shareholders sometimes have to be patient waiting for the rewards to feed through in sales and profits.

It is admittedly more difficult for smaller companies to succeed in this area as tech products often involve much research before they come to market and they need constant subsequent research to avoid becoming out of date rapidly.

This commitment of resources is naturally a greater strain on a small company with limited funds and it can be harder to persuade clients that a small company can produce more sophisticated products than a large one.

Nonetheless, there is scope for smaller companies to find niche markets where a high degree of specialisation produces results. As always with companies in niche markets, it is important to consider whether they are too dependent on one product or one country or both.

Case study: Pace Micro Technology

Pace Micro Technology carved out a niche for itself supplying the black boxes that allow television viewers to receive digital channels.

Pace sold 343,000 set-top boxes a month on average in the second half of 2007 compared with 325,000 a month previously. Pre-tax profits leapt to £15.4m over a seven month period compared with only £4.9m over the previous 12 months.

Chief executive Neil Gaydon claimed with some justification that Pace had strengthened its position as the leading digital TV technology company with new and existing customers, delivered new products and technologies and increased market share in key areas such as high definition TV.

Ambitious Pace announced its intention to acquire the set-top box and related business of larger rival Royal Philips Electronics in a bid to become the world's leading set-top box technology company.

Pace realised that it needed a bigger market than the UK alone. In particular, it needed to sell in the much larger and technologically more advanced US market. This has been achieved, with sales to the US satellite market proving particularly strong.

North America, where Pace supplies over 40 operators, including the two largest pay TV operations, DirecTV and Comcast, now accounts for 58% of sales, with the other 42% split between Europe and Australasia.

One disadvantage of being comparatively small in the high-tech world is that a correspondingly large proportion of revenue must be ploughed into research to stay ahead of the game and into larger levels of stock to meet increased demand.

Over the second half of 2007 the amount of cash tied up as working capital increased from £30.5m to £58.4m. Only £3.4m of the increase came from extra inventory; the big leap was in trade debts, by £49.8m, caused partly because Pace was obliged to allow its new customers 52 days on average to pay for the products against 46 days previously.

That meant Pace ended 2007 overdrawn by £12.1m despite having £11.9m cash in the kitty only seven months earlier.

However, Pace's ambitions were undiminished and in 2008 it agreed terms to buy the set top box division and a related business from electronics giant Philips for about £68m, mainly through an issue of shares that would give Philips a 21.6% stake in Pace.

Chart 16.7: Pace Micro

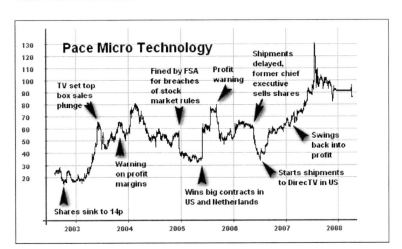

Pace shares rose from 35p in the middle of 2006 to a peak of 131p in just 12 months. They were suspended at 91.25p during negotiations on the acquisition because of its large size.

Key points

- Where a company has basically just one product, it is a massive advantage to become the world leader.

- The UK market for technology is quite small compared with the US, easily the largest market in the world. It is not easy to compete in the US against US companies but it is clearly a massive advantage to carve out a market there.

Case study: Mediasurface

Mediasurface develops and supplies software for handling the content of company websites.

It is an area that has grown enormously over the past decade and most companies quoted on the stock market and many private ones now have websites. Companies quoted on AIM have been obliged to have their own website since August 2007. Websites are now seen as an important publicity and marketing tool.

The growth of this business has inevitably attracted plenty of competition but it is quite a specialised area and is therefore ideal for a small niche business. Although it is the kind of work that many companies prefer to handle in-house, so they can design and control their own systems, these may not match the quality of a site designed by experts in this field.

Mediasurface aims to provide websites, e-commerce sites and internal network services using familiar desktop tools that can operate with heavy usage without depending on significant technical resources.

Customers range from drugs giant Astrazeneca and Dutch life insurance group Aegon to the London Borough of Tower Hamlets and the Welsh Assembly.

In June 2007, Mediasurface bought UK-based web content management supplier Immediacy as a springboard to its next phase of growth.

Mediasurface's main product, Morello, was launched in 2004 and there is no disputing that it has sold well. However, such products take time and money to develop while sales and revenue are built up gradually, so Mediasurface raised £2m by floating on AIM in August that year.

Mixed trading

Former government minister Francis Maude joined the board as a non-executive director at the same time, bringing with him contacts in the public sector. High-profile appointments can persuade potential customers that the company is of some standing, although appointments of politicians who will clearly not be a leading part of government again do not always work.

In the year to September 2004, turnover was still only £5.4m and the company made a small loss but in the following year sales grew 42% and a small pre-tax profit was achieved.

All was going smoothly until October 2007 when Mediasurface stunned the market with a profit warning and the shares slumped. Figures released the following February showed that turnover was up only 5% after stripping out the effect of the Immediacy acquisition, and there was a pre-tax loss of £1.75m.

Morello had a mixed year. Having enjoyed a profitable first half, reporting significant wins at the Foreign and Commonwealth Office and Office of Fair Trading, it found the second half more challenging as the launch of a new Microsoft Office system, which affected Morello, proved more disruptive than expected.

However, the group had £1.8m in cash at financial year end compared with only £1.1m a year earlier so there was no immediate worry of financial difficulties. In addition, it raised £750,000 by placing 15m shares at 5p each, just above the prevailing stock market price.

Chart 16.8: Mediasurface

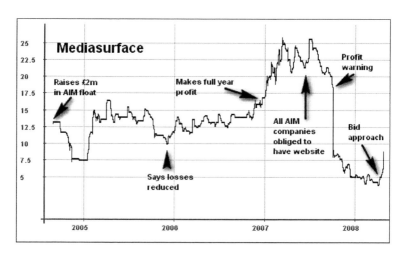

Like many small young companies, Mediasurface has had difficulty in persuading the stock market to take it seriously. The shares bobbed around the 13p float level for two years before the move into profit sent them to a peak of 25.5p in 2007.

Share price movements tended to be erratic, given the thin level of trading in the shares, and when the profit warning came they plummeted from 18p to 8p in one trading session.

The shares drifted as low as 4p but news that a share placing had been made at 5p pulled them off the bottom.

Key points

- Even with promising products it can be difficult for small tech companies to make their mark. Meanwhile share prices, especially for penny stocks, can be quite volatile.

- Small tech stocks can be badly affected if they depend on another company's operating system.

Case study: Netplay

The transformation of Stream, a small telecoms business, raised the question of whether it would be better for new management with different skills to take the company in a new direction.

Stream operated a number of services including specialist fixed-line services, mobile banking and mobile gaming but it was loss making and in November 2006 it decided it stood a better chance as a quoted company if it took a change of direction.

Martin Higginson, who had founded another tech company called Monstermob, made an approach that the existing Stream directors felt would offer a brighter future for Stream.

Monstermob specialised in providing a vast range of ring tones that could be downloaded onto mobile phones. However annoying these might be to fellow passengers in crowded commuter trains, there was no doubt that there was a demand from those who wanted a distinguishing jingle so they knew their own incoming calls from the rest of the herd's.

Monstermob had a short and chequered life. Higginson rightly saw that the UK audience was relatively small and he spotted the opportunity to take his idea to China, where mobile telephony was only just taking off and the potential market was vast.

Unfortunately the Far Eastern promise was only just beginning to turn into reality when the Chinese authorities, alarmed at the way its citizens were becoming hooked, changed the rules and effectively smashed up Monstermob's market.

On the credit side, Higginson was good at spotting opportunities and had the nerve to go for a big prize. On the other hand, he had not covered himself in glory at Monstermob, even if that was not entirely his fault.

Stream's directors gave him the benefit of the doubt and they persuaded the shareholders to do likewise. Higginson was installed as chairman and chief executive and Stream was renamed Netplay TV, turning itself into an interactive gaming company.

Netplay launched TV Bingo in July 2007, giving customers the chance to play via the TV, internet and telephone. Once again, Higginson had seen an opportunity. The smoking ban in Scotland has chopped attendances at bingo halls there and the extension of the ban to England and Wales would inevitably have the same effect.

Thanks to Netplay, smokers could now play from the comfort of their own homes without contaminating other players.

Netplay already ran a roulette TV channel and it decided to introduce blackjack and other internet games.

Chart 16.9: Netplay

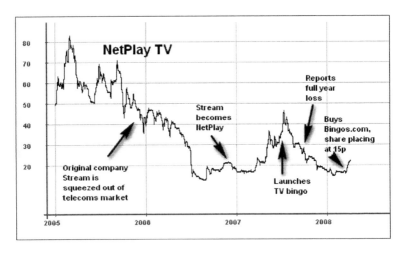

Investors were not entirely convinced that Higginson had a magic touch. Stream shares were trading around 20p when he took over and although the reborn Netplay surged to 46p in July 2007 they were back to 15p by January 2008.

Key points

- It can take a long time before a loss making company is completely rehabilitated. The City is slow to forgive and having a new chief associated with a previous failure hardly helps.

- Changing the name of a company does not necessarily mean that it has put the past behind it.

17.

The Importance Of Management

Top quality management is clearly important to any business but it is particularly vital in the case of smaller companies.

It is much harder for a small company to retain good quality staff in every layer of the business. There may be no clear career path for aspiring staff as there is with a large company spread across different product or geographic areas. Promotion prospects are fewer.

Right at the top, the smaller company will not be able to afford to compete with multinationals on salaries for chief executives and finance directors. Nor will it have the same pull for prospective non-executives. An ambitious director will naturally gravitate to a larger company.

Incentive schemes for executives tend to be more attractive at larger companies where the scope for driving the share price higher makes share options highly lucrative.

Nonetheless, small companies can and do sometimes attract highly talented individuals, who relish the greater freedom that a smaller company can provide. There is greater scope for knowing all areas of the company and its key staff. The chief executive can thus have a far greater control over the ins and outs of the business.

They have greater scope to manoeuvre as they avoid the harsh spotlight of the press and the City. They are less likely to be looking over their shoulders at what their predecessors did.

Chief executives of smaller companies may be the founders of the company. They have the added drive of feeling that the business is their baby and they will feel any success or failure personally.

Because there will almost certainly be fewer shares in issue, they have the opportunity to take a sizeable stake in the company without incurring excessive costs so that their interests are aligned with those of other shareholders.

However, there is equally the danger that a small company becomes too dependent on just one person. The inability to attract top notch non-executives can mean that there is no one who dares to say no to the man in charge when he makes the wrong decisions.

Before investing in a small company it is worth taking a look at how long the current team have been in charge and whether any are approaching retirement age. Continuity at the top can be vital for a small company.

Also check what stakes the directors hold. Have they made a real commitment to the business?

Case study: Majestic Wines

Tim How decided in March 2008 that he would step down within 12 months as chief executive of Majestic Wines, the remarkably successful company that he founded and subsequently floated on AIM in 1996.

One might originally have thought that How would prove an unlikely role model for aspiring chiefs of small companies. He launched his career at frozen foods retailer Bejam, a company whose management was badly caught out when much smaller Northern rival Iceland launched an audacious takeover for Southern-based Bejam. Despite mutterings among affronted southerners, Iceland with its more go-ahead management prevailed.

Perhaps How learnt vital lessons from the experience. Certainly he saw a great opportunity when he snapped up the Wizard Wine chain, which Iceland decided did not fit in with frozen foods outlets and was quite happy to offload it.

Majestic was formed in 1991 and by the time it was floated on AIM in 1996 it was already making its mark, so there was considerable demand for shares from the outset.

Majestic succeeded in the face of intense and increasing competition from supermarkets in addition to existing off licence chains such as Threshers, Oddbins and Unwins. It opened large stores in non-prime locations with car parks and sold wine by the crate rather than the bottle. It also made a virtue of offering fine wines.

The outcome is that the average customer spends more than £130 per visit to a Majestic outlet rather than the few pounds that passes over the counter in most off licences. Majestic's own figure is up from £84 when the company floated, a reflection of how the company has developed its niche.

Total sales have risen from £40m in 1996 to £200m and annual profits from £1.2m to £16.2m.

Apart from paying close attention to detail, How has crucially recruited good people around him to form a highly professional retail and management team. His successor as chief executive will be chief operating officer Steve Lewis, who joined Majestic straight from university.

Chart 17.1: Majestic Wines

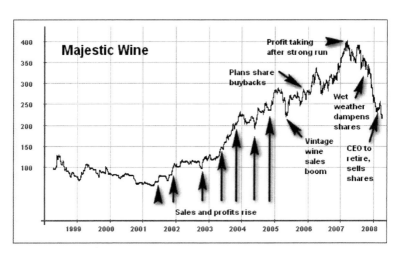

Majestic Wines shares soared from 55.5p in April 2001 to a peak of 402p six years later. Over the next few months many investors took profits as How's retirement approached and the slide was given a further push when How and his wife sold 200,000 shares at 250p each within days of confirming his departure.

Key points

- Chief executives with a point to make are often highly motivated.

- Building a good management team that will keep the business going when the chief steps down is vital. Businesses are better if they do not rely on just one person.

- A successful business model will generally build on its success over a long period. In this respect, a small but growing company offers a better investment opportunity than one that is already well established.

- Watch for warning signs that the shares are in long-term decline as the eventual departure of the key executive approaches.

Case Study: Carter & Carter

The fate of vocational training group Carter & Carter is a tragic tale of what might have been.

The group organised apprenticeships on behalf of the government's Learning and Skills Council. It was named New Company of the Year in 2005, when it floated, and founder Philip Carter received the accolade of Entrepreneur of the Year in 2006 in the PLC awards.

By April 2007 the shares peaked at more than 1250p, giving a stock market capitalisation of £526m.

Chart 17.2: Carter & Carter

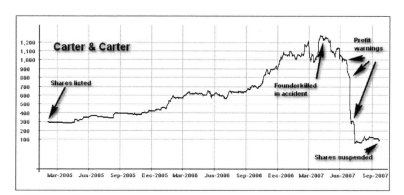

Then Philip Carter was killed in a helicopter accident returning from a football match and the shares started to slide. Three profit warnings followed, culminating in a statement in October 2007 containing the frank admission that the company "could not accurately assess its financial position".

The shares were suspended that month at 82.5p and rescue talks with lenders began. At the end of January 2008, net debt stood at £86m but shareholders were warned that borrowings were expected to peak at £175m and they agreed to waive the company's borrowing limits in a desperate attempt to keep going.

Carter & Carter hoped to strike a deal that would swap some of its debt for equity but it proved impossible to restructure the company to the banks' satisfaction at a time when credit generally was very tight.

Administrators were called in during March 2008. It was unlikely that there would be anything for shareholders once debts had been paid off.

Key points

• Small companies can be vulnerable to unexpected events. When a company is tragically robbed of its top executive, shareholders should immediately consider getting out. While the company may survive, it is hardly likely to thrive without its driving force and it could well find itself rudderless.

- Bankers, suppliers and customers may have put their faith into the company's founder. Once he or she is gone, the company will be in a weak bargaining position if it runs into difficulties.

- Companies with large debts are particularly at risk in these circumstances.

Case study: Theo Fennell

Upmarket jeweller Theo Fennell set up the business that bears his name. After attending art school he joined ancient silversmiths Edward Barnard by chance and found his vocation working with silver in traditional craftsmanship.

He opened his first shop in fashionable Fulham Road, London, in 1982 and the company expanded rapidly as he produced jewellery, timepieces and silverware. To use the company's own descriptions, his distinctive and inspirational style "subtly combines sleek modern designs with a hint of classical tradition".

Others described his work as idiosyncratic but perhaps that was meant as a compliment, because Fennell soon doubled the size of his shop and extended the workshop. After four years he had a custom-designed flagship store built in Chelsea a few doors away. He continued to work from there with an in-house design team and craftsmen in the studio and workshops.

The output can now be seen around the UK with a store in the heart of the City of London and concessions in Harrods, Selfridges and Harvey Nicholls. Theo Fennell is also established overseas in Hong Kong, Dubai, Bahrain, Russia, Kazakhstan, Dublin and the Caribbean.

Celebrities such as David Beckham and Elton John can be counted among the customers.

Importance of a strong team

This is clearly a people business and while Fennell had a back up team the inspiration was entirely his. He did not, however, have a magic wand, or the necessary business experience, and after joining AIM in 1996 the company ran up a series of pre-tax losses in what it described as difficult trading conditions until the tide turned around Christmas 2001. The opening of the new shop at the Royal Exchange in the City in November that year could hardly have been timed better.

The appointment of Barbara Anne Snoad, retail director of Cartier and formerly with another top class jeweller Asprey Garrard, as managing director the following April meant that someone with appropriate experience could look after the business side of things while Fennell could concentrate on what he did best, designing and making jewellery.

The company was then soon able to attract Gavin Saunders, former UK finance director for Tiffany & Co., as finance director.

Even then, profits fell short of expectations in the 2002-3 financial year but at least the company was still in the black and was selling more year-on-year.

The impact of the new management team started to be felt and profits began to take off, although Theo Fennell remained heavily dependent on Christmas trading in common with other jewellers and it continued to make losses in the summer months until 2006.

When Snoad stepped down at the end of 2007, Pamela Harper was appointed chief executive, bringing with her 28 years of experience spanning Burberry, Escada, Hermes, Alfred Dunhill and Jaeger. Richard Northcott, who was in at the inception of the company, remained in his long standing role of chairman.

With experienced management running the business and Fennell in charge of the production side, it was no surprise that trading was strong over Christmas 2007. Although the impact of lower City bonuses was being felt, sales were still ahead of the previous year.

However, a bombshell was dropped in February 2008. Theo Fennell stepped down as a director, plunging the company into uncertainty although he remained as "an ambassador for the brand" and a "design influence".

Chart 17.3: Theo Fennell

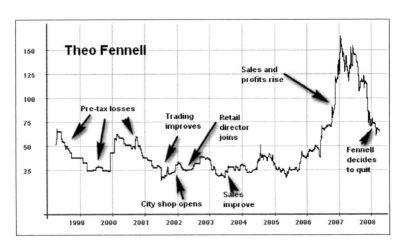

Theo Fennell shares failed to capture the imagination until the middle of 2005. Despite occasional upward surges, they kept settling around 25p.

Increases in profits finally started to tell and the shares shot up to 164p over an 18-month period to January 2007. As so often happens on the stock market, this leap was overdone and eventually the shares fell back to a more realistic level just above 70p by early 2008.

Interestingly, Fennell's decision to step back from the business was taken very calmly by investors, possibly because the shares had already fallen back so far but also partly because the City took the view that the business was now bigger than just one man, however talented he may be.

Key points

- Stock market quoted companies need to be bigger than just one man, however talented he may be in his particular field. The skills needed to run even a small quoted company are quite different from those involved in actually producing the goods.

- The genius behind the business may actually be holding it back. It may be seen very much as his or her private fiefdom rather than a publicly owned company. Is anyone else actually taking crucial decisions that affect the future of the business? Is the founder too thinly stretched?

Family Firms

Many family firms have prospered on the stock market despite the potential drawbacks of trying to maintain a dynasty. Some of these companies are among the largest: Rupert Murdoch has attempted to groom members of his family to take over his News Corp media empire and son James is growing into his father's shoes.

Two other examples of family firms made good are among the UK supermarkets. Sainsbury was still led by a family member until the 1990s. Ken Morrison ran and expanded his family's chain until one deal, the takeover of Safeways, overwhelmed him.

Family firms are, though, usually smaller establishments and they do have some advantages. Often there is a strong leader who has built the business and knows it inside out. He or she will be highly committed.

Such a company will come to the stock market for money to expand and it is then possible for investors to share in the success story – while it lasts.

The main problem with family firms is the succession. Who will take over when the founder and driving force wants to retire, or possibly dies while still in harness?

If there is a family member waiting in the wings, then it will he harder to recruit able executives, as they will see their route to promotion cut off. Also the next generation of family members may not produce a sufficiently talented heir.

Family shareholdings tend ultimately to get split up among different branches of cousins who subsequently fall out or disagree on strategy. Those not actively involved in running the business may want to cash in their investments. Internal family strife may have a detrimental effect on the running of the company and share sales can depress the share price.

On the other hand, if there is no one to pass the business on to, the founder may gradually lose interest.

Case study: Moss Bros

What is it about shops that attracts families? Perhaps it is the fact that a family member can be left in charge of the first shop while the founder moves on to the second.

Certainly retailing has seen its fair share of family businesses and menswear group Moss Bros, perhaps most famous for hiring out formal wear, is no exception. Indeed, there were two founding families, the Mosses and the Gees.

While the chain found its niche in the days when it was truly a family firm, it has struggled to find a place in a modern world where most people who attend formal dinners now tend to own the right rig.

After several years of up and down trading, Moss Bros received a bid approach from Icelandic investment group Baugur, which had already built up a 29.9% stake and had two seats on the Moss board. Baugur proposed to offer 42p a share for the remaining 70.1%.

One Moss Bros board member, Mark Bernstein, dissented with the decision to allow Baugur to look at the books and Michael Gee, a former Moss Bros director and a member of one of the founding families, tried to find the cash to buy out most of Baugur's stake at 50p.

The Gees already owned 8% of Moss Bros while the Moss family was sitting on a stake of about 19%, so the Mosses and the Gees had the ability, if they voted together, to prevent any takeover being made by the increasingly popular method of a scheme of arrangement, which needs a 75% vote in favour.

Michael Gee also threatened as an alternative to call an EGM to try to oust chief executive Philip Mountford and install new management.

As manoeuvrings continued, with retail chain Laura Ashley building a stake of more than 6% in Moss Bros in several stages and reports emerging of possible rival bids to the one from Baugur, Moss Bros revealed another pre-tax loss and followed up with a further decline in sales. Rowland Gee, another family member, sold shares in the market, Baugur dropped its bid and Moss Bros Chairman Keith Hamill retired. The shares understandably continued to slide.

Chart 17.4: Moss Bros

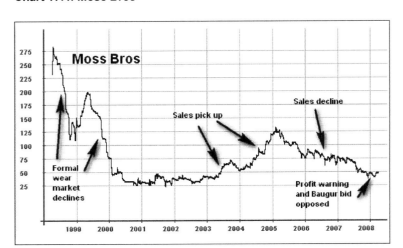

Moss Bros shares peaked at 279p in 1998 but fell all the way to 25p to November 2000 at a time when the stock market generally was buoyant. Hopes that the problems had finally been addressed propelled them to 124p in early 2005 but it was then downhill all the way to below 40p.

Key points

- Small companies, just like larger ones, need to move with the times. But while a large company has a wider breadth of management expertise to help it to cope, a small one has fewer brains to draw on. This can be particularly true of a family firm where top management is drawn from a small pool.

- Family members will often retain large, possibly controlling, stakes in what they still see as their company. They may not always act as other shareholders would wish. In particular, family members may seek to block takeover offers that private shareholders find attractive. Such behind the scenes wrangling can unsettle or distract management.

- Where supposed rival bidders fail to emerge, any rise in the share price presents an opportunity to take profits or at least to cut losses.

18.

Takeover Situations

Smaller companies are generally more vulnerable to takeovers simply because they are more easily digested. Buying a smaller company does not stretch the financial resources of the predator to the same extent.

On the other hand, it is harder for a small company to take over another one unless it is an even smaller company. There have been cases of small companies taking over larger ones but they are inevitably rare.

This is a very important aspect of investing in smaller companies, as it is arguable that takeovers are far more beneficial to shareholders in the target company than in the company doing the taking over.

Some investors do have a policy of investing in potential takeover targets, although it is rather a scattergun strategy: no one knows for sure where the next bid will come from. However, provided you get it right occasionally takeovers are a way of making profits, possibly substantial ones, in a short space of time.

Look for sectors where there is consolidation, that is where there are a great many companies with small market shares and there are signs that larger companies are buying up smaller ones to try to dominate the market.

Sectors where this has happened have been as diverse as banks, housebuilders, telecoms, plant hire and car dealers.

Where a bid does emerge, investors in the target company need to consider carefully what to do next. Where a bid is purely indicative, that is there is no firm offer on the table, it can be right to sell out in the market, taking a profit. On the other hand, whether there is more than one potential bidder the odds favour holding on to see what emerges.

Remember that if a bid fails, the shares will fall back and in the case of smaller companies a lost opportunity has often gone for ever.

Directors of small companies can misjudge the situation badly. They may have no previous experience of handling a takeover approach and can agree a deal too cheaply or become too greedy and stick out for more than the suitor is willing to pay.

Case study: Styles & Wood

The stock market has been rather unkind to shop-fitting business Styles & Wood but management made a bid approach, confirming that the shares had been oversold.

Chart 18.1: Styles

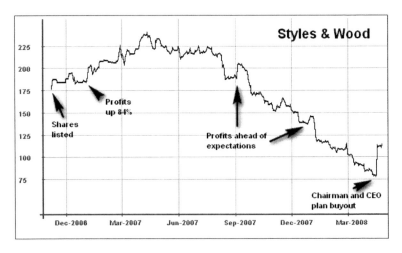

Styles & Wood floated on AIM in November 2006 at 150p and a strong trading performance pushed the shares to a peak of 237p the following April, just after an 84% rise in full year profits was reported.

However, the shares gradually but steadily declined to a low of 77.75p exactly a year later despite a string of encouraging trading updates and profit figures plus the payment of a dividend.

It seemed that investors were worried that the harassed retail sector would cut back on store improvements, although clients such as Tesco continued to do well.

Chairman Gerard Quiligotti, chief executive Neil Davies and other executives backed by private equity then indicated that they proposed to make a takeover offer at 125p a share. While that was well down on the original flotation price, it was markedly better than the prevailing stock market price. Another advantage was the possibility of flushing out another potential bidder.

Key points

- Strong trading is not always reflected in a company's shares. That opens up the way for an opportunistic bidder to try to grab the company at a comparatively cheap price.

- Directors should have a thorough knowledge of the business and be able to spot when the shares have fallen too low.

- Takeover proposals from management usually come with backing from private equity funds. While management know the business, their financial backers almost always insist on carrying out their own due diligence, which means inspecting the books. That does give time for any other potential bidder to come forward.

- It is highly unlikely that management will have got its valuation of the company so badly wrong that the bid falls through. So it is usually right to hold on if the share price remains below the proposed bid price.

Case study: Regent Inns

How Regent Inns shareholders must regret the day that their bars and clubs group set out to buy rival Urbium.

It was June 2005 and, buoyed by trading that was running ahead of expectations, Regent contacted Urbium with a proposed bid of 820p a share, an approach that was quickly rejected as being too little.

That moment proved a turning point for Regent, which hoped that combining the two businesses would create a group with three strong market leading brands and a portfolio of premium West End and City bars.

Duplicated costs could be removed and Regent would have more muscle in negotiating terms with its suppliers.

Regent owned outlets under the names of Walkabout and Jongleurs while Urbium had Tiger Tiger.

Regent did come back with a higher proposal worth 975p in cash and shares but its approach had alerted other potential bidders with more financial muscle to prospects at Urbium.

Finally, Regent walked away after receiving a second rebuff and private equity fund Electra came in with 1,075p, a whole £1 more than Regent was prepared to countenance.

How things go wrong

Perhaps the episode, although lasting less than two months, was too much of a distraction for a Regent Inns team that had been performing pretty well up to that point. Perhaps the Urbium deal was needed to shore up Regent as trading became increasingly difficult.

Whatever the reason, Regent went on to demonstrate that when things go wrong they tend to go very badly awry.

While Inventive Leisure, owner of the Revolution bars chain, was also snapped up by private equity before the year was out, Regent was starting to struggle.

Although press reports of late night binge drinking suggested that this ought to be a growth sector, other factors were imposing constraints. Business rates and rising employment costs were taking a toll, licensing reforms created uncertainty and the looming ban on smoking in public places threatened to drive way some drinkers.

Regent implemented a number of changes at some inevitable expense ahead of licensing reforms that took effect in November 2005. These included increased door security (bouncers in popular parlance), a reduction in the maximum numbers allowed in, longer trading hours at some bars and the introduction of plastic glasses and bottles.

Regent still cherished hopes that it would play a role in the consolidation that was taking place in the sector but in April 2006 a rise in its share price forced an announcement that the company had received an approach that could lead to a takeover offer for itself.

In the event, the talks were terminated in June but this was a distraction at a time when trading, as Regent subsequently admitted, had been difficult since the New Year. Overall, like-for-like sales for the year to 1 July 2006 declined by 0.4%, even though the England football team did the decent thing and waited until the last day of Regent's financial year to get knocked out.

Effects of an acquisition

Undeterred, Regent quickly snapped up Old Orleans, a portfolio of 31 themed restaurants across Britain, for £26m. It argued that 'Regent Inns' skills and experience in this marketplace will deliver a greater focus on the future development of the Old Orleans brand'.

Another claim was that the Old Orleans business would benefit from being a significant part of a smaller group rather than an insignificant part of a larger group, Punch Taverns.

Investors were entitled to doubt whether this would be the case, although it was true that some of the current directors and senior management of Regent Inns had experience of managing the Old Orleans outlets when they were owned by Scottish & Newcastle up to 2003.

Firstly, what effect would there be on morale at Old Orleans at being passed on twice in three years? Secondly, if the highly successful expanding Punch chain could not make a go of Old Orleans, why would Regent be able to do better? Thirdly, would themed restaurants fit in with the Walkabout TV sport bars and the Jongleurs comedy clubs or was Regent dividing itself among too many ideas? Finally, was Regent right to take on more debt, having previously decided not to pay a dividend in order to reduce existing borrowings?

The acquisition was completed in September 2006. In the meantime, the existing Regent outlets had been through another couple of months of difficult trading with hot sunny weather favouring the great outdoors, particularly as there was no big sports event to bring in the punters.

The late night market continued to be highly competitive, with pubs able to stay open longer since licensing deregulation.

Regent management now found itself tied up in integrating the Old Orleans chain, recruiting 'an operational management team with a proven track record'. What was that about Regent already having experience of Old Orleans in a previous life? This was the first we had heard about the need to recruit management.

The diversification into a chain that was primarily about eating rather than drinking also meant that a "food development executive" had to be found.

New electronic tills and back office systems had to be introduced at Old Orleans so it fitted into the existing group.

Warning signs

Interim results to 30 December 2006 contained warning signs. The increase in turnover for the previous six months was down entirely to the acquisition of Old Orleans. Sales at the existing chain were actually down. So, too, were operating profits.

Still there was no dividend as Regent needed the cash to invest in the Old Orleans outlets and set about reducing debts again.

It was not until the end of May 2007, though, before shareholders had to be weaned off the diet of optimistic pronouncements to which they had become accustomed. A trading statement at that stage contained a hidden profit warning.

It is usually a particularly bad sign when a trading statement begins with a phrase such as 'an encouraging start to the period' and ends with a grudging admission that profits will fall short of expectations.

Not only had trading deteriorated but two Old Orleans outlets were closed for extensive refurbishment and were thus going through a period of incurring extra costs while producing no revenue.

Recovery in trading in the other Old Orleans businesses was meanwhile slower than expected. Investment in a number of key areas, including minor refurbishments, staff development, site maintenance and further refinement of menus were delayed.

Chart 18.2: Regent Inns

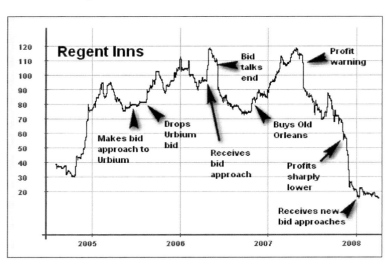

Regent Inns shares were trading around 80p when the ill-fated attempt to buy Urbium was made but they moved up to a peak of 118p in mid 2006 and again 12 months later on hopes that Regent itself would be taken over. In both cases the shares soon fell back sharply.

Worries over trading pushed them below 20p at the start of 2008.

Key points

- Companies that launch an offer but find themselves outbid by a stronger rival have a tendency to lose their way subsequently.

- Where a company turns down an approach it is worth considering whether trading conditions are likely to get better or worse. This will help you to decide whether to take a profit by selling on the stock market or stick with the company.

19.

Doing The Splits

Breaking up is hard to do according to a 1960s pop song and so it can also be in the world of business. Managements of large companies are rarely keen to see their realms divided up. They naturally want to be big fish in big ponds.

However, over recent years the idea that large conglomerates would do better split into bits has grown in popularity.

Companies that are split off from stock market companies because they are deemed to be peripheral to the main business can be a fruitful source of investment. Often the existing shareholders in the main group will be allotted corresponding holdings in the part that is spun off.

Company executives can be as prone to fads as the rest of us and thinking goes in cycles. Building a wide ranging group comes into fashion. The argument is that a more widely spread set of businesses is better able to ride out a downturn: if one bit is affected, the rest of the operations will see the whole group through.

Cross selling becomes a buzz word. Customers taking goods or services from one part of the operation can be sold complementary products from other parts of the empire.

Then the prevailing wind switches to the opposite direction. All the talk becomes about core and non-core businesses. Operations on the fringes are spun off as separate entities on the argument that they will fare better under separate, dedicated management rather than being lost in a large organization.

Analysts have become very fond of doing what is called a 'sum of the parts' calculation. They work out what they reckon each part of a business is worth and add it all together. If the total is more than the stock market capitalisation of the entire business then, so the argument goes, it would be better to break up the group into bits.

As with all stock market fads, this is all highly debateable and the valuations are subjective, but there is no doubt that some subsidiaries of larger businesses do better standing on their own. And such is the perversity of the stock market, many of them are subsequently taken over by another conglomerate at an inflated price, to the great benefit of their shareholders.

Biffa

One prime example was waste disposal company Biffa. It grew up within the Severn Trent water group at a time when utilities were diversifying away from the regulated water supply business, where prices to consumers had been brought under control by the industry regulator.

Biffa was split off as a separate entity in October 2006 with the share price initially around 262p. It declared a maiden interim dividend of 2.1p in December that year followed by payouts of a final 4.2p for the full year to 31 March 2007 and an interim of 2.3p for the following six months.

Two private equity funds approached Biffa in September 2007, when the share price was 250p, over a possible offer for the company. Eventually, in February 2008, Biffa agreed to be taken over by a consortium led by Montagu Private Equity at 350p a share.

So in the space of 16 months Biffa shareholders had received 8.6p in dividends and seen their shares gain 88p each, a total return of 37%.

Often the spin-offs become private companies, bought by managers backed by private equity. If they are later floated on the stock market, they should be treated with some suspicion, as the original backers will undoubtedly have got the best of the bargain and are seizing their chance to cash in while the going is good.

Always check if they have been loaded up with debt while in private hands. If so, has the debt been used to grow the business or to line the pockets of the original investors?

Debt has to be serviced, that is the interest paid and the debt gradually paid off. So consider whether earnings are sufficient to cover the interest payments comfortably. Ultimately, if not immediately, interest will have to be paid before dividends.

Where a non-core company is immediately quoted on the stock market, it is more likely to be worth considering as an investment.

Case study: Homeserve

One example of a highly successful spin-off came at water supplier South Staffordshire, which like other water companies had toyed with branching out into vaguely related business concepts only to change its mind.

In South Staffordshire's case, diversification took the form of a 75% stake in a company called Homeserve that provided householders with insurance against water leakages and breakdowns in domestic appliances.

Homeserve's selling point was that it provided an emergency service, sending out staff to carry out the necessary repairs at a time when finding a decent plumber was becoming increasingly difficult.

South Staffordshire argued that the regulated water services offered less scope for improving profits than the bit that had been tacked on so the minority holding in Homeserve was bought, giving 100% ownership, and the water utility was split off.

The demerger of South Staffordshire and Homeserve in April 2004 was a double bonus for shareholders, who found themselves with stakes in both companies. Within six months the water company was taken over by AquaInvest, a Bahrain company, at £11.20 per share compared with a stock market price of £6.57 immediately after the demerger.

Homeserve has proved a less spectacular investment but a profitable one nonetheless. It has grown partly through successful trading and partly through a series of acquisitions to move up to the ranks of mid-cap companies.

Chart 19.1: Homeserve

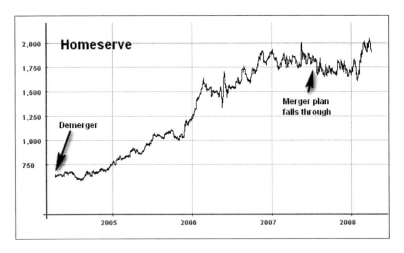

Its shares traded around 650p in the early days after the demerger but subsequently settled around 1750p in 2007. Shareholders who got out at the peak of 2,000p in May 2007, when Homeserve looked set to agree a highly attractive merger with household goods insurance specialist Domestic & General, trebled their investment.

Lessons to be learnt

- Sometimes the part of the business being split off has better prospects than the main business. In the case of utilities such as water companies, profits may be restricted by the rulings of the industry regulator while the peripheral parts are unregulated.

- Small companies split off from larger ones are quite likely to be subsequently involved in a merger or acquisition.

Case study: Emap

Media group Emap was once one of the largest companies in the country. Having started life as a regional newspaper group called East Midlands Allied Press, it built up into a newspaper, national consumer and business magazines, commercial broadcasting and exhibitions group.

Within the stable of the now London-based group were FHM and Closer magazines and radio stations Kiss and Magic.

As such, it was a fine example of how a small company can transform itself into a giant to the benefit of shareholders.

However, more recently the movement was in the opposite direction and by selling off parts of the empire and splitting its operations Emap gradually turned itself back into a smaller company.

Towards the end of 2006 Emap was still in expansion mode. It won a commercial radio licence for Liverpool and paid £19m for Trades Exhibitions, a family-owned organiser of exhibitions in the professional beauty sector.

But as stockbroker Collins Stewart subsequently remarked, Emap's strategy started to look as if the company had 'lurched from one expensive foray to another in search of growth'. The downturn in advertising that affected other media groups such as ITV and Trinity Mirror was taking its toll.

Irish radio stations were put up for sale and as it became clear that Emap would have to be split apart and the chief executive, Tom Moloney, quit abruptly in May 2007.

Irish radio went for £135m in July, quickly followed by the sale of 50% of Box TV, Emap's music TV business, to Channel 4 for £28m. Exhibitions businesses in France and Australia were also sold, slimming the group even further.

Four days later Emap put everything that was left up for sale, saying it was prepared to consider offers for the whole group or for any parts of it. In the event, no one wanted the lot and in December 2007 Emap sold its consumer magazines and remaining radio interests for £1.14bn with the promise that £1bn would be returned to shareholders.

Emap was thus reduced to its business-to-business communications unit organising trade exhibitions, festivals, conferences and awards, supplying information and publishing business magazines.

Chart 19.2: Emap

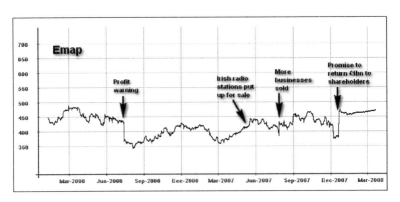

With the shares trading at around 760p, including the 461p promised special dividend, the Emap rump was valued at just under 300p a share or about £650m. However, there was even better news for Emap shareholders.

Rival media group Guardian Media, backed by private equity firm Apax Partners, came up with a £1bn offer for what was left, a premium of nearly 60% over the stock market capitalisation, so Emap shareholders eventually received a total of about £2bn including the special dividend.

Key points

• If the various parts of a business are not fitting well together, it can be highly lucrative for shareholders if the business is split into bits. That can be true even where the group specialises in operations that seem to fit well together.

- The rump of a business that has been split apart is extremely vulnerable to a takeover offer, which can be well above the stock market valuation.

- Splitting up businesses can often mean a sizeable special dividend as the remaining shrunken business will have little use for any cash pile it ends up with.

20.

Slippery Slope

Just as ambitious companies can make it into the big time, big and well established companies can stumble badly.

Large companies may become small because of a long period of decline. It is rare for a big company to hit the buffers and collapse overnight but they can suffer a painful lingering fall from grace over many years. The problem may be within the company or the sector in which it operates or, most likely, a combination of both.

The question for investors is to decide whether the company is in terminal decline or ripe for rejuvenation.

Declining companies tend to see their share prices gather downward momentum. At first investors are reluctant to believe that a large company, especially one with a well known name, can possibly fail. Then as disillusion sets in the shares collapse in on themselves.

There are many opportunities for nimble short term traders to make quick profits as each fall is followed by a small and temporary blip upwards but this is a high risk strategy because it is so easy to get the timing wrong. On the whole, unless you have a spirit of adventure it is best to hold back until there are genuine signs that the company is recovering. Some basket cases do not come back.

It is comparatively easy to spot when a particular sector is in difficulties as most or all of the companies in that sector will be suffering.

Housing sector

For instance, the housing sector fell out of favour in the middle of 2007 as the shock waves of the US housing collapse started to be felt over here. A period of free-for-all mortgage lending, boosting house prices to unaffordable levels, followed by rising interest rates is a recipe for a sharp downturn in demand for new homes.

Consequently all UK house builders saw their shares and their stock market capitalisations fall over several months. It was also possible to work out the most vulnerable: those such as Taylor Woodrow with operations in the US where the collapse in house prices was more severe and builders simply shut up shop in many parts of the country.

That was a case of an entire sector in temporary decline: no-one doubted that the UK housing market would recover again in due course given that pent-up demand for housing continued to outstrip supply – even more so if house builders cut back on their building programmes until selling prices recovered.

There was a great opportunity here for patient long-term investors to buy smaller house builders and wait for the recovery, with the consolation that in the meantime these companies were paying attractive dividends.

Car dealers

Other sectors are likely to suffer in harsher economic times. Car dealers are a case in point. This is a sector that moves forward or goes into reverse on a broad front. If individual drivers decide to hold onto their cars longer before trading in for a new one then the new car market obviously suffers.

Dealers are forced to resort to providing incentives such as discounts on new cars or inflated prices for trade-ins. Although in theory the second-hand market should benefit from reduced supply pushing up prices, it tends not to work that way. The same factors that are keeping buyers out of the new car market are also keeping less well off motorists out of the second-hand market. So profit margins on resales are also under pressure.

At the same time, cash-strapped companies will be cutting back on vehicle purchases, making those car fleets last four years instead of three.

As with house builders, some car dealers will suffer more than others. It tends to be the middle market that feels the squeeze. Buyers at the top end are more likely to be able to afford luxury cars – there are always people with money to burn even in a recession – while less well off drivers have the option of trading down to something cheaper.

These are two examples of sectors suffering a temporary setback. It will often be possible to spot the most oversold companies or the ones with the best recovery prospects.

Retailing

More problematic is where the negative factors are more deep seated as in the retailing sector. Retailers have for some years been caught in a squeeze between rising costs and consumer resistance to rising prices as online competition grows.

Retailers are major employers of low paid staff so they are heavily affected by increases in the minimum wage; they own large properties incurring spiralling business rates; they transport goods using ever more expensive fuel. Meanwhile, online retailers can offer goods at lower prices because they do not carry such heavy overheads.

As always, some retailers have rallied more than others. Some have found a niche market; some have slimmed down by closing poorly performing outlets.

This sector requires investors looking for bargains to consider which companies will come through relatively unscathed and which are doomed to eternal struggle.

Self-inflicted problems

In contrast, there are companies that have dwindled through their own mistakes rather than from a general misfortune. Who would have thought that a major electronics manufacturer such as GEC, which at its zenith had £3bn sitting in the bank and a share price top side of £10, could be transformed into a small cap in the space of two or three years?

GEC, later renamed Marconi, paid over-inflated prices for acquisitions in the dotcom arena just before the dotcom bubble burst. It spent the £3bn kitty and ran up debt of £4bn at a time of rising interest rates, lumbering itself with a debt burden that could not be serviced by the meagre earnings from the mistimed acquisitions.

In the end, the banks took control of Marconi and the shareholders were wiped out.

Similarly, construction and buildings management group Jarvis was an architect of its own misfortune. Anxious to compete in the growing public/private finance market, where private companies took on government and local authority projects, Jarvis tendered for school building contracts at prices that proved unprofitable.

In addition, some local authorities baulked at paying, claiming that work was substandard.

Caught in a cash squeeze caused by a shortfall in revenue and expensive remedial work, Jarvis became the target of well publicised claims that contractors were not being paid on time. So suppliers became reluctant to continue to support Jarvis unless payment was up-front, which intensified the cash crisis.

As with Marconi, there were a number of short-lived opportunities to make money from short-term buying and selling of Jarvis shares as they rose briefly after each sharp drop. Also as with Marconi, Jarvis shareholders were effectively wiped out, leaving the banks owning what was left of the company.

Case study: Woolworths

It is hard to think of former high street giant Woolworths as being a small company but it has become one as far as a stock market is concerned. It even suffered the ignominy of becoming a penny stock.

It is hardly a small company by conventional standards. It has more than 800 high street and out of town stores with a total selling space of 7m sq feet. Its 30,000 employees also work on an internet catalogue, the wholesale distribution of books and home entertainment and audio-visual products.

It still had turnover of almost £3bn in the financial year to February 2008.

However, profits have been harder to come by as Woolworths has been affected by factors afflicting all retailers as well as some of its own.

The retail outlets themselves continued to operate at a loss until the autumn of 2007 despite repeated earlier assurances from the company of imminent profitability.

In April 2008 Woolworths bowed to the inevitable and slashed its total dividend for the 2007-8 financial year by two-thirds.

Changing times

The cheap and cheerful image of Woolworths no longer fits into the modern world, where rival chains such as Next and Marks & Spencer have brought down the price of higher quality goods and others such as Primark and Peacock have cornered customers seeking bottom-of-the-market bargains.

Founded in the UK in 1909 as the offshoot of an already well established American store chain, Woolworths eventually became independent before being merged into the Kingfisher chain and then being spun off to regain its independence as a listed company in 2001.

Woolworths has chopped and changed over several years, for example introducing and then scrapping its Big W superstores. Despite some successes, most notably the Ladybird children's ranges, it has failed to find a new niche. Nor does it have the spending power to tackle larger chains head on.

Meanwhile, the high street has grown increasingly competitive and online sales are taking away shoppers. All retailers have had to divert cash into revamping stores to retain the attention of their customers.

Woolworths has, a little belatedly, launched what could be a successful online and catalogue arm making use of its stores as collection points. This could rescue the group but it will take time.

Market caps can provide a useful reminder that even well known names can effectively become small companies as far as investors are concerned.

Woolworths shares peaked at 55p in March 2005 on a takeover approach from private equity fund Apax Partners, which dropped its proposal after looking in detail at the Woolworths accounts. At that point Woolworths was valued on the stock market at just over £800m.

The dividend has since been raised in an unsuccessful attempt to shore up the share price but investors inevitably fretted as it became increasingly obvious that the payout could not be maintained in the face of falling underlying profits.

Chart 20.1: Woolworths

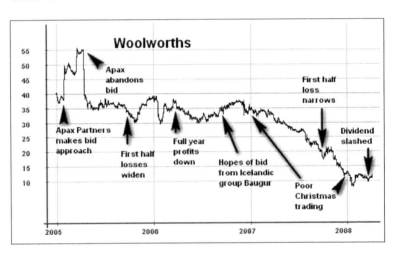

The shares slumped to 8p in January 2008 after reports of another poor Christmas in the retail outlets. With 1,459m shares, Woolworths had a market cap of just £127m at that level.

No further takeover offer had been forthcoming despite hopes that acquisitive Icelandic group Baugur would step in and the shares have struggled to hold above 10p.

Key points

- Companies that have fallen on hard times often have difficulty in coping with their changed circumstances. Management that have presided over the decline tend to be slow to adapt and they continue to operate as if they were still running a big company.

- No one likes to admit that they got it wrong and that applies particularly to macho management. It often needs new executives to come in and make a fresh start if the company is to recover.

- Profits may have slimmed down but the overheads probably have not. A company in decline may well have a large staff to pay and lots of property to finance.

- Putting things right is likely to be expensive – just at a time when the company could do without more costs. Reducing staffing levels involves redundancy payments immediately to save wages in the future. Vacating property involves breaking leases or finding a buyer.

- A period of decline is likely to affect staff morale, especially when the P45s start to appear.

- If the share price is propped up by a high dividend payment, investors need to consider whether the dividend can be maintained.

Case Study: Pendragon

The fall from grace of car dealer Pendragon has been truly spectacular. This was the company that fought and won a macho takeover battle for smaller rival Reg Vardy in 2005-6, threatening in the meantime to launch an offer for Lookers, another car dealer that attempted to outbid Pendragon in the fight for Vardy.

Car dealerships are still a highly fragmented business, despite some consolidation in recent years. Chains tend to be of just a handful of outlets in a small geographic area.

Dealers are thus very much at the mercy of the car manufacturers because of their lack of bargaining power – each dealer forms a very small part of each manufacturer's sales and franchises can easily be switched elsewhere.

Pendragon seemed to have broken the mould. With nearly 400 sites offering more than 30 brands of cars, commercial vehicles, trucks and motorcycles it is the largest dealer in the country. However, it is not large enough to be immune from considerable pressures that have affected the entire sector.

At the AGM in April 2007 the company told shareholders that it was selling fewer used cars and was making less profit per vehicle. Two months later came a profit warning.

The actual figures, released in August 2007, showed a drop in pre-tax profits from £51.5m to £33.5m for the six months to 30 June. Chief executive Trevor Finn admitted that motor dealers faced a challenging time.

Nonetheless, he raised the interim dividend by 38%, from 1.45p to 2p, and boasted:

> *These conditions offer a market leader like Pendragon many attractive growth opportunities. We expect to identify further opportunities as smaller competitors seek to exit the market.*

It is true that tough times provide an opportunity for ambitious companies in a fragmented sector to pick up weaker rivals who lack the financial strength or willpower to continue. In fact, the previous week Pendragon had bought 19 dealerships.

Linking dividends to profits

However, investors should always beware of being seduced by a dividend increase in these circumstances. The results were announced in early August when the credit crunch was just beginning to bite.

If life was tough in the first half, it would hardly be any better in the second half. Less confident consumers could easily postpone the purchase of a new car or go for something cheaper. Likewise businesses feeling the pinch could make fleet cars and vans run longer.

Despite Pendragon's acquisitions, total revenue had grown by less than 3% year on year, a warning sign. In November 2007, the group admitted that operating profit would fall £12m short of market expectations. The new car market was proving competitive, with dealers undercutting each other and reducing profit margins.

Although it claimed that some recovery in margins was taking place, Pendragon said it was taking a more cautious outlook for 2008 and it expected operating profits for the new year to fall £18m short of previous hopes.

Chart 20.2: Pendragon

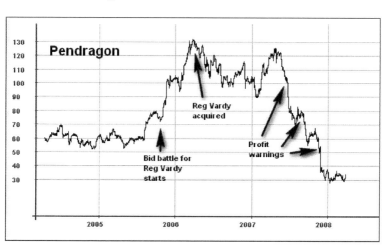

The shares peaked at 132p in March 2006 and, after sliding to 90p, rallied again to 125p in April 2007. Then it was downhill all the way, including a sharp fall after the November profit warning, before they found a floor at 30p in early 2008. They had thus lost more than three-quarters of their value in nine months.

Results for 2007, released in February 2008, confirmed the bad news. While turnover remained static at £5.1bn, pre-tax profits halved from £97.7m to £46.5m.

Chief executive Trevor Finn put on a brave face, saying:

As interest rates rose last year, the car market became progressively more competitive, putting pressure on used car margins. We acted early, closing poorly performing sites and, as a result, are better placed to face the challenges in what remains an uncertain market in 2008.

Key points

- When a large company falls on hard times the downturn tends to gather momentum. Overstretching resources, especially by overpaying for acquisitions and running up expensive debt in the process, leaves a declining company struggling.

- Although it may be reclassified in the FTSE indices as a Small Cap, a company in decline may retain many characteristics of a large company, including large turnover and employee numbers, plus ownership of a number of sites.

- It is a dangerous game trying to judge when such shares have hit the bottom and are ready for recovery. Large companies that have shrunk may find it difficult to cope with their new status and are likely to resort to panic cuts that damage recovery prospects or to sit it out until the market turns.

Index

888 135-137

A

acquisitions 57-58, 86, 114, 202
active investors 102-106
administrative expenses 53
ADVFN 22, 41, 76
AGM 40-41
AIM, see 'Alternative Investment Market'
Air Partner 139-142
Allen plc 35
Alternative Investment Market (AIM) ix, 5, 9, 10-13, 17
    delisting from 14
    dividend yields 79
    fees 11
    moving to the main board 12
    performance of 27-28, 75-76
    requirements 11, 39, 48
ambition 37, 113, 119
annual general meeting, see 'AGM'
annual report 48
assessing companies 47-49
Arbuthnot Securities 44
Argus Research 45
Asos 55-57, 70-71, 85
assets
    current 67, 71
    fixed 67
    net 68
awareness 108-109

B

C

G

GEC, see 'Marconi'
Gladstone 12
goodwill 67
    impairment 58
government contracts 126, 128-129
green investments 129-130, 132, 135
group accounts, see 'consolidated accounts'
Growth Company Investor 46
Guinness Peat Asset Management 102
GW Pharmaceuticals 61-65, 71-74, 85

H

Hardide 90
Hardy Oil & Gas 12, 153-154
Hargreaves Lansdown 46
Hemscott 41, 46
Homeserve 187-188
Hornby xiii-xiv, 57, 88, 121-123
housing sector 193-194

I

iBall, see 'Interactive Investor'
ICAP xiii-xiv
III, see 'Interactive Investor'
illiquid shares 19
Imagesound 15-16
income xiv
    statements 48-49, 51-66, 78-79, 108
        examples of 56, 63
Independent 43-44, 46, 76
independent auditor 56
Independent International Investment Research 45

S